Reflections on A Changed Life

Laure L. Wang
王樂怡

Laure is writing the book with Dynavox.

Prologue

Laure Wang was born on January 14, 1971 in Kingston, New York, the dutiful eldest daughter of a dad and mom. When she was fifteen, her mother tragically passed away. Laure threw herself into her studies and earned a coveted entry to Stanford University, Goldman Sachs and Harvard Business School, and eventually co-founded her own private equity investment company in 2005. On the personal side, she married her best friend and fellow investment ace, Kabir Misra, in 2004. In 2010, she was happily working and living a full life in Hong Kong with Kabir and their two beautiful sons, four-year-old Marat and four-month-old Madyn. But like every good story, there is always a plot twist. On April 26, 2010 at the age of 39, Laure suffered a severe brain-stem stroke. After surviving two days in a coma, she was diagnosed with locked-in-syndrome, a condition where her mind was clear but she was unable to speak or move - a mute quadripalegic. This is the story of her journey.

Contents

Part One

Reflections on A Changed Life

Part Two

Part Three

Part Four

Part Five

Part Six

Part One

Chapter 1: Falling ill

I don't remember anything - not the how, not the coma, not the rush of visitors. My stroke was at the base of my brain, caused by arterial ripping and depletion of oxygen to the brain. I woke up paralyzed and mute, or in medical terms "a mute quad." I was a prisoner in my own body. I could not talk or move below the neck. I was diagnosed with locked-in syndrome. A syndrome that I had read in The Diving Bell and the Butterfly. A syndrome is an inadequate word to describe when one's whole life has been ripped away. I had ups and downs from depression to despair.

"Stroke" had never been in my vocabulary, as it was associated with being overweight or old, of which I was neither. My husband, Kabir, later told me that I had complained of a migraine the night prior to my stroke. The next day, I fainted during a meeting at the office. Rebecca, my colleague, rushed me to Queen Mary Hospital. In Hong Kong, Queen Mary is considered to be a good public hospital. But somehow they did not know what was wrong with me. If they had diagnosed my stroke earlier, the damage might not have been as severe. Timing is everything....

Chapter 2: Hong Kong

The night before what people politely call the accident, I was grilling meat and drinking soju (Korean rice liquor) at Arirang, a local Korean eatery in Hong Kong. Who knew my last supper would be with Janice and Joe Bae, the head of KKR Asia and Yana and Stephen Peel, the head of TPG Asia. Dining with two private equity titans was common when the expatriate community was so small. Who knew I would be a mute quad typing with my eyes the next day? Have you ever thought about what you would eat for your last self-fed meal?

A massive dose of a drug called heparin given early could have minimized the damage, or possibly killed me. Oh how I wished they had used heparin. Anything was better than this. Selfishly I wished I had died. But I wanted to stay alive for Kabir and my two sons, Ton Ton and Caillou. At the time of my stroke, Ton Ton was four and Caillou was a mere four-month-old.

Chapter 3: Lability

Lability happens when you cannot control your emotions. Usually you cannot stop laughing or crying, no matter what the circumstances, however inappropriate. Once, at a church sermon, I burst out laughing and could not stop despite the hushed silence. Kabir and my caregiver, Annie, had to wheel me out from the nave. Another time, I was crying out of frustration at the opera. My caregiver, Yolanda, had to take me out of the dark and quiet auditorium. The opera staff mistakenly called the paramedics because they thought something was wrong. Lability became a convenient excuse for nervousness. Lability became my easy excuse when I had an inappropriate response. I could hide behind lability. When I heard about my friend's daughter's death, I could not stop crying. Sometimes I had to cry to stop laughing. If I cried about my situation, it could be hours.

Chapter 4: Dignity

You don't get much dignity as a mute quad. You get caregivers who clean and give you baths, but when you are wiped, you lose independence and identity. Your unending refrain is "don't treat me like an animal or an inanimate object," because that is how you feel. Even when caregivers are nice, you feel bad when you can't communicate with them. It's probably the hardest thing to get used to with locked-in syndrome. You have a clear mind, but since you cannot express it, people treat you like you don't have a frontal cortex. What is the difference between a human and an animal?

Chapter 5: Food

For one year, I subsisted on a bland canned liquid food channeled through a tube into my stomach. My friend, Steve, introduced me to Vitamix, an industrial quality blender which enabled me to get  rid of canned feeding. Food was supposed to be fun and therapeutic. But for one year due to the weakness of my tongue, things had to be pureed to the consistency of crème brulee or flan- basically they were unrecognizable. Think baby food. Kale, organic fruits and vegetables were blended and shot directly into my stomach. Foie gras was one of the few foods I could eat without alteration. I dreaded July 2012 with trepidation as this is when foie gras was banned in California. By 2012, I graduated to chopped food. Nutrition became an obsession. Grass-fed beef or pastured eggs were important, as was my weight. These were the only things I could control.

Chapter 6: Music

In the beginning, I hated all music. The psych at the hospital thought my hearing had become extra sensitive post-stroke. The reality was Norah Jones had been played over and over on my iPod to the point where I could not stand it. Norah Jones would cause storming, a form of seizure where my pulse would go very high. I preferred silence.

Chapter 7: Faith

Why me? That was the big question. I often asked the question, -"Why did this happen?"- Faith gave me hope and was lacking at the same time. I was both grateful and mad. Why wouldn't the omnipotent one heal me? Pastor Joanie read scripture to me that helped me a lot by giving me hope. She spent hours talking to me and meticulously spelling out what I wanted to say. I relied on my faith to stay alive. Luke 5:17-26 was particularly special because it gave me hope.

'On one of those days, as he was teaching, Pharisees and teachers of the law were sitting there, who had come from every village of Galilee and Judea and from Jerusalem. And the power of the Lord was with him to heal. And behold, some men were bringing on a bed a man who was paralyzed, and they were seeking to bring him in and lay him before Jesus, But finding no way to bring him in, because of the crowd, they went up on the roof and let him down with his bed through the tiles into the midst before Jesus. And when he saw their faith, he said, "Man, your sins are forgiven you." And the scribes and the Pharisees began to question, saying, "Who is this who speaks blasphemies? Who can forgive sins but God alone?" When Jesus perceived their thoughts, he answered them, "Why do you question in your hearts? Which is easier, to say, 'Your sins are forgiven you,' or to say, 'Rise and walk'? But that

Kabir, Marat, and Madyn getting baptized

you may know that the Son of Man has authority on earth to forgive sins"—he said to the man who was paralyzed—"I say to you, rise, pick up your bed and go home." And immediately he rose up before them and picked up what he had been lying on and went home, glorifying God. And amazement seized them all, and they glorified God and were filled with awe, saying, "We have seen extraordinary things today."'

Luke 5:17-26

Chapter 8: The Setback

I had a CT scan two years out which showed my pseudo-aneurysm had grown, and a new one had formed also. The doctor didn't know why, and I ended up fearing all illness because I thought my hard work would be negated. It was debilitating to my motivation since I worked so hard to live, yet I might die anyway. In the end, it was a mistake, and I realized I had to be more vigilant in my own care, and I could never give up.

Chapter 9: Dibya

Dibya was my domestic helper in Hong Kong. She knew me for five years pre-stroke, before I was defined by my disability. My new world was being handicapped, wheelchair access, handicapped parking, elevators and private rooms so people would not stare with pity. They didn't know the real me. I was more than my disability. My condition got me good parking but that was all. I treasured Dibya because she knew me as a whole person. When she fled surreptitiously in the middle of the night, I was devastated. I felt that I had lost myself. None of my other caregivers knew me pre-stroke. To them, I was just a mute-quad. I had no hope of being the old me again. In a way I had to mourn a death. The death of me.

Chapter 10: Aqua Therapy

My therapist, Deborah, had advocated warm water therapy as a way to recover. There was a story of a paralyzed man in Maui that had been buffeted by warm waves for days who became better. In Palo Alto, we found the Betty Wright Aquatic Center which had a warm water pool. At first when I was brought into the water, I was immobile. I was disappointed to inadvertently hear Joanne's comment about my lack of movement in water. I thought I was doomed. My caregiver, Vanessa, has diligently taken me to aqua therapy every week. I can now move and am working on walking.

Chapter 11: Mood Swings

I had mood swings from elation with my kids to suicidal thoughts. I needed an outlet but was forever being told to think positive. How could a prisoner who had bottled up her feelings for three years be positive? I needed to grieve the loss of my old life- a life as a jet setting foodie in her prime.

Chapter 12: Privacy

You never have a private moment. You need to get used to your bodily functions being in plain view, and your every conversation being three-way. When people ask for a private moment, what they're used to is a privilege. Privacy is not my reality.

Chapter 13: Larry

Larry was my house manager, but really his job couldn't be defined. He was my voice and arms and legs. I was incredibly grateful yet jealous. The better he did, the more it high-lighted my deficiency. One time while watching "Horton Hears a Who," Caillou wanted Larry instead of me. I was happy for the kids but sad for me. Larry provided a normal childhood for my kids. He had great bonding with my kids, particularly with Caillou, who only knew me as a mute-quad. I felt more of a bond with Ton Ton, because he knew me for four years before my stroke. I appreciated Larry, but I also viewed him as competition for my kids' affection. I always felt torn when Larry wanted to take Caillou for some new experience, because Caillou would remember Larry instead of me. I wanted Caillou to have all the experiences, but selfishly, I wanted him to have them with me.

Chapter 14: Dynavox

The Dynavox was a system that allowed me to type with my eyes. The system wasn't very user-friendly, and it would take me days for just a few sentences. That's why it took me over two years to write this book. Many a session with Dynavox was spent crying and sweating. I was grateful for a voice, but I hoped for one less frustrating.

Chapter 15: Direct Communication

Always having to spell makes you very terse and direct. Spelling with one less letter can save valuable time and energy. You're labeled as rude when you don't have tone, and don't spell "please" and "thank you". It hurts to feel mean when you have no intention of being mean.

Chapter 16: Needs

I had emotional and physical needs, but for about three years, I had only focused on the physical. I put priority on therapy, to the exclusion of my happiness. People focused on my physical needs, and because there were so many, my emotions took a back seat. Now was the time to shift the scales. I wanted to focus on intellectual stimulation, working, and joy. I cut down on therapy to focus more on my psyche. I wanted to recover mobility, but I also realized I couldn't wait to be happy. Happiness had to be in the present, even though I was still disabled. I always put the needs of the kids and Kabir ahead of mine, but now I had to focus on me. I made a joy list, which included going to Muir Woods, Stinson Beach, lectures, concerts and plays.

Chapter 17: A Dear Friend

I had a longtime friend from Stanford. He was very depressed by being unemployed for one year, and he had had brain surgery. I always tried to help him get a job and by listening to him. He couldn't make a decision and was always negative about himself. He was my dear

friend, but I couldn't be his therapist. Once after I talked to him, I even vomited from stress. I realized I was only physically disabled not emotionally disabled. My disability was easier to deal with than one not visible. One could see my defects but not his. You could see a wheelchair but not depression.

Chapter 18: Madyn

Madyn, nicknamed Caillou, is my youngest son. He was only four months old when I had my stroke, and he is now four. I sometimes lament that he only knows me as a mute quadriplegic. I hope he knows that I love him. I hadn't spent his infancy with him but now got joy from passively watching him. I want to have interactive playtime with him, but instead

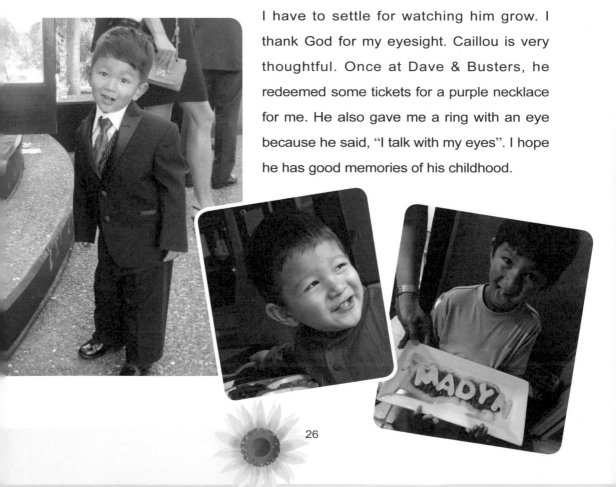

I have to settle for watching him grow. I thank God for my eyesight. Caillou is very thoughtful. Once at Dave & Busters, he redeemed some tickets for a purple necklace for me. He also gave me a ring with an eye because he said, "I talk with my eyes". I hope he has good memories of his childhood.

Chapter 19: Marat

Marat, affectionately known as Ton Ton, is my elder child. He always caused me worry because he was four when I had my stroke and coma, and I thought he was angry with God. I wanted to have someone to explain why his mommy had been taken away. He was very cerebral, and he could easily touch me. Once he gave me a bracelet of rubber bands. He said it was elastic because

his love was unconditional. He was so caring for me. I loved going to the movies with him. I miss my time with him. I used to do a lot with him, and I want to hug him.

Chapter 20: Kabir

Kabir is my husband and best friend and rock. I always felt bad for him, because his life has changed. He could have left, but he always makes me feel safe and strong. With his love, I feel I can do all of my painful therapy. I couldn't live without him. My love for him was the same as it was pre-stroke. He is strong, because he loves me even though I am different now.

Chapter 21: Disneyland

I had an epiphany on my trip to Disneyland. They treated me like I was the old Laure again. I got to ride all of the rides without lines. Every ride was wheelchair accessible, and the staff was super nice. I never felt rushed or that I didn't belong. I had to be transferred into rollercoasters, drop zones, water rides and every other attraction. My caregiver, Vanessa, and my nanny, Berta, made my trip successful.

It was the first time I saw my disability as an advantage, and it didn't define me. My whole world opened up since I had no more fears. I also got to bond with my boys. It was Madyn's first time and Marat's second time to Disneyland, so I got to make special memories with them. After this breakthrough, I could contemplate commercial flights and cocktail parties, all of which I used to avoid. I went to Disneyland again the next year, and my experience was just as great. Now I had found my own personal happiest place on earth.

Part Two

Chapter 1: Victory

Victory sounded so final. Most people defined victory as walking. For me victory meant happiness. Victory sounded like the end, but for me it was just the beginning. Now things were how-to and not if. I imagined flying commercial to eat macaroons in Paris or swimming in Bali. My whole world opened up, and I could see myself doing it all. My victory had just begun.

Fannie and George's Valentine's Day Bash

Chapter 2: Labels

When I thought of myself, it was always as a mute quad. That was what the doctors said when I first had had my stroke. I believed I was paralyzed. But my spinal cord wasn't severed. I wasn't paralyzed just weak; weak in muscle fibers, and weak in nerve signals. I learned to avoid labels. Everyone was different. I was just weak.

Chapter 3: San Diego February 2014

The first two days at Legoland were another good amusement park experience. I was only turned away from one ride, but I could handle the disappointment. My kids had just seen "The Lego Movie" for the second time so they loved it. We stayed at The Legoland Hotel, so I got to see their imaginations run wild when building bayonets and space cruisers. The third day I got to catch up with an old friend from Hong Kong. I realized many people didn't define me by my disability but treated me the same as before the stroke. There was Erin, Jean, Chris, Elizabeth, Kyung, Betty, and the list went on and on. I was blessed with love outside of my family. I also met Waleed, the founder of the Neuro-Ifrah approach. On the spot this brain whisperer said he would treat me. I also got to go on the beach, something I had eliminated from my reality. Because I was now able to hold my head over 1.5 hours, I knew my next trip could be involving a flight. Overall, San Diego was great, and I could see myself traveling again.

Chapter 4: Gifts

My biggest constant has been my perseverance. Going to Stanford, getting into Harvard, starting my own company, and now for rehabilitating, I needed to be determined and have a reason to live for myself. Despite fatigue or sickness, I always tried hard. I was relentless in pursuing my recovery. God has given me the gift of perseverance; I know I can be healed, because His nature is healing. I didn't have fear that I wouldn't recover, and I took my gradual progress, from taking my first steps to being able to move my thumbs as evidence.

Chapter 5: Saison

Every now and then, it is good for the soul to have ladies night out. Saison was one of those posh restaurants with a prix fixe menu in San Francisco. Jean, Erin, Verna and I decided to meet at Saison for dinner. Over pigeon and wine, I laughed so hard that my abs hurt the next day. I have known these girls for over twenty years, and I really know their essence. What I realized was most people have too many distractions and no time for themselves. I, on the other hand, had no distractions and all of the time in the world for me. Who was luckier…?

Chapter 6: My First Flight

I wanted to test myself and see if flying commercial was viable. With my grandmother's memorial service in LA, I had had a bittersweet opportunity to try a short flight. I was most nervous about sitting upright for a longtime, but because of the San Diego trip, I knew it was possible. San Francisco airport was very organized; I sailed through TSA security to pre-board before anyone else. I had been told by my  therapist, Michelle, that the bulkhead row had more room to transfer. I brought my own wheelchair down the gangway and then transferred to the airline's impossibly narrow aisle chair. The service was very nice, and I was grateful for the chance to say good-bye to my grandmother.

Now my next trip could be Kauai, Hawaii, for my tenth anniversary.

Chapter 7: Value

The more I could accomplish, the happier I was. But ironically I also felt more grief. I wanted my accomplishments to have come earlier. The more I knew was possible, the more I thought I had wasted energy on anything that delayed my goals. Now I had more fear, because there was more to lose. Life finally had value. In the early stages of my recovery, I only lived for my husband and kids. Now I had joy back in my life.

Chapter 8: Reflection

Every four weeks or so, I had my mani-pedi at home. Since I didn't move much, my polish could last longer than the usual. At first, I would only request clear polish for my hands and red polish for my toes. My nails were a reflection of my soul. For three years, my mood had been

Halloween Nails 🎃 👻

dominated by monotony, practicality, and caring about what others thought was reasonable. Now my nails are pink, green, orange, and purple. Today I have yellow nails with a glittery blue tip and the party finger has the opposite, glittery blue with a yellow French tip. My soul is dominated by whimsy, fun and joy. I could care less about the opinion of others. My next mani-pedi is purple nails with pink tips, and the opposite for my toes.

Chapter 9: Betrayal

Caregivers are your friends, your voice, and your most intimate advocate. One of my caregivers had been with me for four years. I let her sons sleep over with my kids. I thought she was my most empathetic caregiver. But when she quit, she didn't even say goodbye. I realized my dependence on her was mistaken. I thought she cared about me, but apparently I was wrong. There was no depth of feeling, I was merely a job she could walk away from. What I realized was that everyone was different, I could not presume anything. I could've concluded that I should only depend on myself, but I didn't believe everyone could be so selfish.

Chapter 10: Advantages

Once I went for cocktails at the Rosewood Hotel, and I spotted A-Rod. After a few sips of my Cosmopolitan, I was able to muster the courage to take a picture with him. I couldn't have asked for a nicer first celebrity sighting. A-Rod was great and gracious. I realized I didn't need much courage. After all who can say no to a woman in a wheelchair? I became bolder and my mantra became "If you don't ask, you will never get."

Chapter 11: My Sanctuary

For the last two years, we temporarily moved to another house so I could rebuild our old house to meet all my new access requirements- like an elevator and wider hallways for my wheelchair. Although I had not consulted a feng-shui master, I knew the house had good energy, because I always felt like I was on vacation when at home. Thus, I took the opportunity to perfect my sanctuary. I chose every tile, every light fixture, and every flower. Even my elevator was custom and was modeled on the lift at the Legoland Hotel, complete with a multi-colored globe and the music "Everything is Awesome." I designed a secret tunnel between both boys' rooms, because I wanted to encourage closeness between brothers. Nothing was an accident.

Chapter 12: Vina

I had a therapist that made me realize many of my muscles worked but were only weak. She gave me hope. The first time I moved my arms, back extensors, and abs were all thanks to her. I believe God sent me a healer, and it was Vina. She was trained in the Neuro-Ifrah approach like Waleed. Over 90% of the videos I posted showing my progress were taken in her therapy sessions. I am grateful for Vina and all the more hopeful for Waleed.

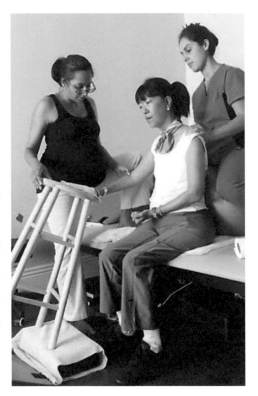

Chapter 13: Will

I always believed I should sublimate my will to God's will, but I believed that when I said, "Thy kingdom come, thy will be done," it was always a test for me to see if I could let go of my will in favor of God's will. I always erroneously thought God's will was negative. Could I accept the deaths of Kabir or my kids, or could I accept God if He would never heal me? I realized His Kingdom on earth was to be like heaven. No suffering, no death, no tears in His Kingdom. I wouldn't have a stroke, and everyone I loved would be there. I lost all fear. And I wasn't afraid anymore, because I wanted God's Kingdom, and His will, because I believe God is good.

Chapter 14: Hildy

Hildy was my psychologist who came every week. She helped me reach a lot of conclusions in my journey. Hildy suggested a joy list of things that I wanted to do. I diligently ticked through Muir Woods, the beach, plays, operas, and symphonies. I needed to be happy not for others, but for me. After about two years, I felt all my sessions were my recounting good times. I didn't feel the need for her. I was in a better place. Whereas I used to be holed up in bed, now I loved going out, shopping at the outlets, taking the boys to school, seeing movies, trying new restaurants, and traveling. I was happy, and I no longer needed an emotional crutch.

Chapter 15: Spiritual Growth

At first I was sad, filled with self-pity and depression. Life was not worth living except for the safety of the kids and Kabir. But because of my faith, I made it through my suffering by becoming stronger and better. I could have become bitter and victimized. But because I knew I was loved by God, I had hope and a positive mentality. When I reread my old journals, I could see how prayers were answered and my issues solved. It was not easy but because I knew the future was good, I could be happy and I knew I only had upside. God has made me a better person, and away was the old angst and fear. I like the new me more.

Chapter16: Family

When I first had my stroke, I craved only nurturing. My mom had passed away when I was fifteen, so my extended family gave me tons of support, from my Aunties Kuei Mei, Sylvia, and Che staying with me in the hospital to my Uncles Neil, Jong, and John giving Kabir a break to be with the kids. Before I had had my tracheotomy closed, I called upon my cousin and ENT

doctor, Calvin, who comforted me about my surgery. My blood circulation was poor, so I was always cold, and my stepmother, Su Ah-Yi, gave me beautiful and warm shawls. My younger sister Joanie, is my kids' fun aunt who taught them about camouflage and camping. Last but not least, my dad visited every three months, making the long voyage from Taiwan to Atherton. He even offered to pay for Waleed and my tenth year anniversary trip to Kauai. I realized no one could replace my mom, but through a composite of loving family, her role was represented.

Chapter 17: Physical Touch

What I always craved was being able to hug and be hugged. That means I could love and be loved. But since I couldn't move my arms, I could only wait. This made me want to get a pet. I was always trying to solve my needs with alternatives. Since I couldn't get the real thing, my solution was to look elsewhere.

Chapter 18: Growth

When I was well, I did everything at home: All the discipline, parenting and household management. Now that I was sick, there was a vacuum. Only Kabir could fill my shoes, but I had never asked him to play that role before. Now it was trial by fire, and he passed. I was very proud of Kabir's development as a dad, and I could see how the kids loved him. Because of my stroke, Kabir could now experience firsthand the hardest job you could ever love.

Chapter 19: Kabir II

Kabir is my soul mate. We have a common shared experience that makes me feel alive. Once on a business trip, Kabir bought me a book on the life of Alain Passard. Kabir remembered I had interned under Alain Passard in Paris. I could imagine myself being defined not by a mere wheelchair. Kabir also has a connection with me. Whenever I think

of him, he calls, and he is my fastest form of communication because he knows me so well. He has handled a stressful and devastating situation with grace and a sense of humor. He is my support and rock through all my change. I never thought I would test him "through sickness and in health."

Chapter 20: Asia Alternatives

I had co-founded an investment management firm called Asia Alternatives ("AA") in 2006. Melissa M. was my co-founder and friend. She tirelessly gave me support and treated me like the old Laure. Her son, Justin, always gave me a hug. Rebecca X., my other co-founder, was with me when I fainted from my stroke, and she always came to visit me when she was in the US. Aki Y. also came to visit even when I was in the hospital in Chicago. Bill L. respected my contributions to the firm. All

My office building in Legoland

the partners bent over backwards to make me feel normal, and I am appreciative to them in my recovery process. Now even in a wheelchair, I can still work and grow the business. No one at Asia Alternatives treats

me as handicapped. Asia Alternatives taught me I still had value, and stimulation of my brain didn't end with a stroke. I still enjoy working, and I have a legacy to build.

Here is my speech I gave to the team in July, 2015.

"Friends, family, and staff, you all have contributed to where Asia Alternatives is today. As we celebrate our 10 year anniversary, I think back to 2005. I was pregnant with Ton Ton, and Asia Alternatives was only a concept. I remember creating Asia Alternatives' first presentation on Melissa's dining table. At that time, Asia Alternatives didn't have it's name. We code named it Red Sweater. In Jardin House, I built the first Hong Kong office with Monique and Tammy. Bill remembers our first meetings where I had to pump my breast milk for Ton Ton under a cloth. I look back on Asia Alternatives as my baby. Look how it has grown. Next came Valerie in Beijing. She didn't even have three kids yet, only Haywood. Then came Praneet. I remember his giving Ton Ton lots of Ben10 paraphernalia. I had to juggle between two babies but it was worth it. Next came Jin. She used my real estate broker to move from the Bay Area to Hong Kong. Bill started as a consultant and didn't work at Asia Alternatives. Then we recruited Aki. He might be short, but he is a private equity titan. On April 26, 2010, I fainted during a meeting, and Rebecca rushed me to the hospital. I suffered a severe stroke that left my cognitive abilities intact, but I was paralyzed and mute. Even though I haven't met everyone, I still appreciate everyone for making me feel normal. I am thankful my baby is now an adolescent. Nobody at Asia Alternatives treats be like I have a disability and I can still contribute to the adolescence growth. Lastly, I want to thank Melissa and Rebecca

for being the best partners. They always supported me, visited me, and went above and beyond the call of duty. You all are my family and it takes a village to raise a child so let's grow this adolescent into adulthood!"

Chapter 21: Espacio

Every week at my kids' school Sacred Heart, they have an assembly for high school students to reflect on inspiration from their community. It is called Espacio, a Spanish word that refers to time one makes for their hearts to receive God and His love. Brian M, a high school history teacher asked me if I would be willing to open the Espacio

for the 2014-2015 school year by narrating my journey and answering questions from the students. I gladly accepted, because I wanted the students to understand that even someone who had lost the things we take for granted could still have a good quality of life. My spiritual cup is full. I now had a new legacy.

Epilogue

Since writing this book, I have traveled to Hawaii, which was a high and also had to say goodbye to Vanessa, a low. Vanessa empowered me to live and improve. But what I realized was life will always have ups and downs. It is how you embrace them and deal with them that matters. Vanessa will always be my friend, and I was fortunate to have

known her. She won't take away my independence or love of travel. Those things are inherent in me. Life will always have highs and lows. It's how you react to them. Just as Vanessa was leaving, I learned that foie gras again became legal in California.

I envision myself as this traveling dragon. I will travel and walk. I believe I am this dragon, and you should too.

Part Three

Kabir Misra

To me, Laure has always been defined by a) her intelligence and her dedication to work; b) her love of food, wine, entertainment, shopping and travel; c) her absolute dedication to her family and friends, and, d) her ability to manage all aspects of her life and our home – she was the best mom and wife. The last weekend before Laure's stroke was a microcosm of all this:

Laure had got home exhausted from a week of work in Shanghai on Friday night. On Saturday, we spent the whole day with Ton Ton, not really doing much. We went to Toys World in Central, checked out my new office in Wanchai, ate a lot of dumplings at Crystal Jade while Ton Ton opened his new Bakugan, bought some supplies at Watson's and then went home to nap and head to dinner with Laure's friends, where we (again) ate and drank a lot and Laure had lot of fun. It was a relaxing day for me and I met some very fun people through Laure. We spent all of Sunday at Branksome with Ton Ton, discussing Laure's new fund and her role in it, ordering in Thai food from Phukets and I fell asleep while Laure watched 24. On Monday, Laure had the whole morning planned. First, we went to the US Embassy to get Ton Ton's picture updated on his passport, and then, to the immigration department to get his "huishangzen". We stopped at Starbucks and then I took Ton Ton home while she went to the office for an LP meeting. I spoke to her an hour later since she kept all our info and I needed my bank account number. While we were a team – Laure was undoubtedly the captain and ran our whole life.

The amazing thing about Laure is that she never fundamentally changed post her stroke. Yes, she was not herself for a while, but over the last couple of years, she has completely regained her control of our life and her own. It has been awesome for me, Ton Ton and Caillou since no matter how good the agents, the principal is always better. The captain of our team is back after a stint on the disabled list!

On a) and b) above, Laure has begun (despite some challenges) to work and manage our own investments again. She attends all Asia Alt meetings and ICs when possible, went to the Alibaba roadshow lunch and even put Rich Lin through a tough presentation prior to investing in his fund. In my professional life, she continues to be my closest confidant and guide. She is also now shopping up a storm again, is the best customer for Cabi, and has probably every store credit card out there! In fact, the only way to throttle back the shopping has been to make sure that she spends her time eating out at the best restaurants and drinking the best wine – and staying away from the mall or the online stores. She began with soup and purees, then foie gras and the

uni that Masa brought back for her - and now it's everything save the spicy foods. That has given us back the ability to have special dinners together and for her to do dinner dates with kids when I am out for work. So far, Laure has travelled mainly through TV (diligently watching the Anthony Bourdain shows that Ton Ton and I also love) or in her Sprinter Van for short distances, but the Legoland and Disneyland trips opened up her world and we had an amazing trip to Princeville this fall. Next year it's on to Hong Kong! Laure had always believed that the best gift her dad gave her was the gift of travel and she wants to give that to her kids as well. It is the old Laure again – working, eating, drinking, shopping, watching her shows/movies and travelling.

Of course, the greatest strides she has made are with her family and friends. It is a testament to the quality of Laure's relationships that all of her friends have remained steadfast in their support for her and have provided her the companionship and love that have kept her going. Laure, similarly, always prioritizes her friends and craves interaction with them. For some years we had "my friends' and "Laure's friends", and then in HK, "our friends". Now, she also has a whole host of new friends who are critically important to her. It has been fun to spend time with all of the above groups of friends over long dinners where Laure eats, drinks and listens to all the stories! In many ways, this is what she enjoys most now (after the kids, of course) and I wish that we can do this more over time. It is amazing that Laure can hold her own in these dinners and get her voice heard above the din. She is truly interested in each of her friends' lives and wants to stay abreast of how they are rearing their kids, what they are watching for entertainment, where they are travelling to and what they are eating and drinking. Laure seems to partake in their joy and it is wonderful to see her laughing along with them. More importantly, Laure still has her nights and days out with her own friends without the family – and then it is time for me to spoil the kids and treat ourselves to some junk food!

At home, Laure has always been the best mother and wife - she had always planned every minute of Ton Ton's life in HK and unfortunately, was unable to do the same for Caillou initially. Ton Ton could not have had a fuller, more fun and fully developmental first 4 years, and now Caillou is too. Laure had made a big career sacrifice so that she could be the perfect mother and spend a lot of time with - she also insisted that he have a sibling to be with him all his life and devoted the last months before her stroke to carrying and nurturing Caillou. She has overcome the speech limitations that are an impediment to fulfil those responsibilities in the manner to which she was accustomed, and is again in complete control of the children's activities, their academic and extra-curricular lives and the food they eat (or more importantly, the food they do NOT eat). There are regular movie nights with the kids, walks at Stanford, shopping excursions, amusement park trips, museum outings, baseball and soccer games – in fact, both Ton Ton and Caillou know only come to me when they need something to do with fast food, soda and going to watch professional sports! Most importantly, she makes

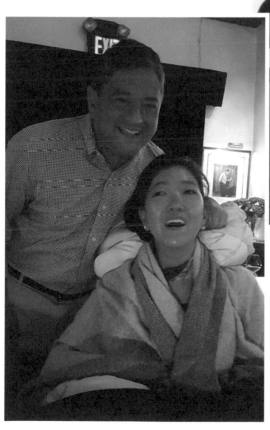

me a better father by making sure I spend time with both kids equally and setting up regular activities for me to do with them both. She is constantly spelling out "DON'T TEASE CAILLOU"....and does want to ensure that he is not left behind. Laure also increasingly manages her own care, all the nannies and the house (that she built by herself). All of the household staff are now used to the 360 degree reviews that she did at Goldman. I am increasingly redundant and again relegated to planning dinners and vacations!

All of the above leads to the most amazing thing I've realized over the last 5 years: Laure is still the same person she was before and after the stroke. She may look different to the naked eye, but at her core, she is the same. She is the best wife and the best mother with amazing instincts for how to develop her children. She is an amazing friend and has made many new ones as a result of the stroke, even as she has remained committed to her old friends. She is a great businesswoman and continues to help Asia Alternatives, her dad and Softbank. She is an excellent planner and manager and continues to be that even today. A lot of folks were lucky to have her in their lives before she got ill and a lot are lucky to have her in their lives now. Most importantly, Ton Ton, Caillou and I have the most critical part of our team back in full form and we look forward to every day for the rest of our lives with the same zest we had before. As Laure tries to get the world to see her as the same Laure, they need only look at her immediate family. We cannot be happier to be together and enjoying our lives again.

Marat & Madyn

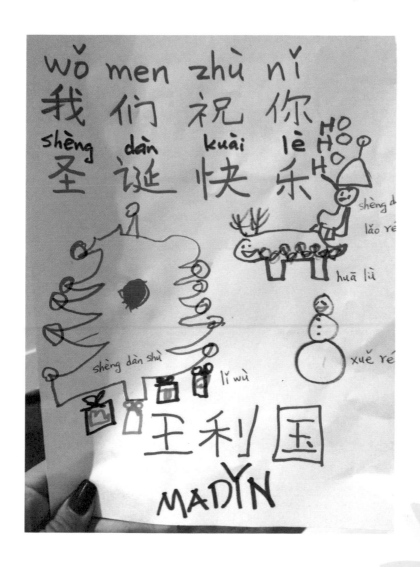

"We miss you momma!"

5

Caillou

Paul Wang

Laure,

Ever since you were young, I knew you are a strong, decisive, and self-motivated person. You knew what you were going to do with my minimum supervision. Though independent, deeply in your heart, you knew that I had been always behind you and loved you with all my might.

As I said in your wedding, you are more than a daughter to me; we are partners in both life and business. I am not just a father to you, either. When you were little, I also acted as a mother. I know both relations were not easy for you because I might not be as attentive as a mother when you needed me most, and you might get a lot of pressure from me when working together. However, you have always been loving and supportive. Later when you started Asia Alternatives and made a successful business in the venture capital and private equity field, I was so proud of you. Even today in your wheelchair, you still hold a strong willpower to life and a great deal of love to family and friends. You made me even prouder to have you as daughter.

Maybe you didn't know, from the day of your sickness I was thinking of you for almost every minute of the day. I prayed to God wishing it

was me who suffered all the pain instead of you. I travelled frequently to see you and kept you company. I searched for all experts and doctors, hoping to find a cure. I never give up in looking for new treatments to help you recover.

Five years went by and I see you making a lot of progress and moving toward a new self. You tried so hard to reconnect yourself to the world. Here I would also like to praise Kabir for his performance and achievement. He takes care of you, the kids, the household, and everything run smoothly. He monitors the kids' education, your rehabilitation, and nanny and caregivers' duties to maintain the family is on track. I couldn't thank him more for his brilliant work. I always tell my friend how I appreciate Kabir for the past years. Because of him, the family is restored.

This year is your 10th anniversary and I am so glad to join you in Kauai to celebrate the event. Seeing you getting better and better, I just want to say, "Hang in there, God is always with you, and so is Dad."

Love you.

Dad

Susan Su

Dear Laure,

I have always thought that you are the kind of daughter that every mother wants. You are smart, bright, brilliant and highly disciplined. You knew your way and headed toward the goal with full confidence. You were tough and self-motivated in work but sweet and considerate to your family and friends. You run the business successfully and at the same time managed your family well. Who could ask more for a daughter like this?

It was really heart-breaking seeing you get sick when everything looked so promising at that time. I could never forget the day when I first saw you in the Hong Kong hospital. I cried with Paul fearing that we might lose you. However, during the past four years, I have witnessed a strong soul reaching out from despair. You made tremendous progress along the path by taking all therapies available. You didn't give yourself up even though the recovery process was full of tears and pain. You couldn't speak and move freely, but this won't stop you from taking care of the kids. I was so moved seeing you attending Ton Ton and Caillou's school events and highly participating in their daily lives. I know you have dedicated every effort to them as a mother.

I was so happy to know that you stepped out further this year,

taking the kids to Legoland and Disneyland. I could see from the picture that you had a great time. Also, thanks to the arrangement of Kabir, Paul and I made the trip to Kauai, Hawaii to celebrate your 10th anniversary and had a great time together. Back to the same place where your wedding was, everyone was touched. I could see the love between you and Kabir and the love among all the family getting stronger. This is because you are such a wonderful daughter, an affectionate wife, and a loving mother to all of us.

Laure, I know you will get better and better each day because you won't allow yourself to be limited. But please don't stress yourself. I love you and may God bless you.

Sue

Reflections on A Changed Life

Joan Wang

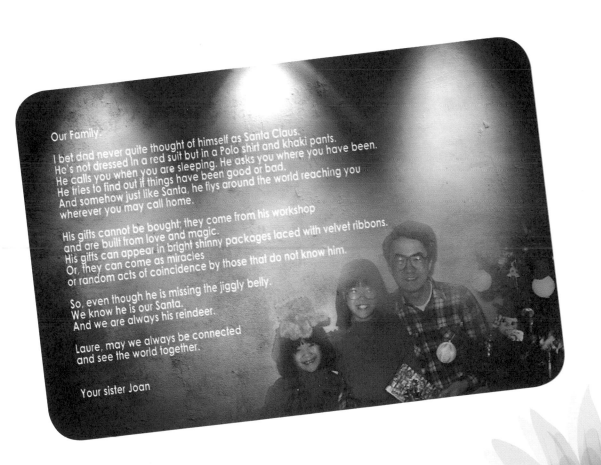

Our Family,

I bet dad never quite thought of himself as Santa Claus.
He's not dressed in a red suit but in a Polo shirt and khaki pants.
He calls you when you are sleeping. He asks you where you have been.
He tries to find out if things have been good or bad.
And somehow just like Santa, he flys around the world reaching you
wherever you may call home.

His gifts cannot be bought; they come from his workshop
and are built from love and magic.
His gifts can appear in bright shinny packages laced with velvet ribbons.
Or, they can come as miracles
or random acts of coincidence by those that do not know him.

So, even though he is missing the jiggly belly.
We know he is our Santa.
And we are always his reindeer.

Laure, may we always be connected
and see the world together.

Your sister Joan

Jong Wang

Dear Laure,

We admire your efforts and perseverance on your magnificent book with such profound meanings. What an accomplishment!!!

We all are very confident that you will continue to rehabilitate at your home with significant progress each day.

We pray you will continue to gain strength, to fight, to heal and to achieve full recovery.

We sincerely admire your high spirit and value of your life and hope you continue to work hard to achieve "victory and happiness" everyday as you wanted.

We will not give up, we are not scared and we will succeed together. Let us go forward and march through the long tunnel hand in hand, and God will surely bring the brightest exit out of your endurance.

Uncle Jong
Aunt Julie
July 15, 2014

Cherene Wang

I remember as a young adolescent, meeting my cousin Laure for the first time since we were children. Being almost 10 years my senior, she was always someone I looked up to. She exuded such confidence and intelligence as she spoke, and her beaming smile always lit up any room she walked into. I, on the other hand, was shy, tentative, and certainly not as eloquent. It was evident that she was going to be something big one day, and I admired her for everything I was not. Her stellar resume was one to be envied -- she completed undergrad studies at Stanford, business school at Harvard, joined Goldman Sachs, and later built her own asset management empire. She became something big indeed. And at her wedding in 2004, I would celebrate among her friends and family, the life love & partnership she found with Kabir. So when I first heard that Laure had a stroke, and the condition she was in, I couldn't help but think that everything she had achieved thus far in her life was meaningless. When I stayed with her for a week in Chicago during her rehabilitation and I witnessed firsthand what the stroke took away from her, it was hard not to think that everything she worked so hard for was gone in a poof, just like that. *But how wrong was I.* For what the stroke took away, her resolve added threefold. The room now lights up not with her beaming smile, but her hearty laugh. Her

eloquence was replaced by something much more valuable, her growing sense of humor and faith in God. And her confidence unmatched, as she has proven time and time again, there is nothing she can't accomplish when she puts her mind to it. Best of all, the friends and family who have rallied by her side to cheer on each personal victory is testament to the fullness of her life. Laure, may you continue to go forward bravely in the knowledge that you are admired more now than ever before.

Sylvia Wei

I am Laure's aunt on her father's side. The first time I heard the news that Laure had a stroke was on April 26, 2010. When I heard the news, I could hardly believe my ears. Only a couple of months ago, she came to visit us in Singapore while attending a business meeting. How could anyone have a stroke at such a young age - not just the kind of stroke older people get but the worst kind, called "locked-in syndrome." Four days later, I was at Laure's bedside at Queen Mary Hospital in Hong Kong. She was unconscious and heavily medicated. Every few hours, her body cramped up uncontrollably like a pretzel, called storming. She was also intubated. The nurse had to come to stick a thin tube down her throat to suck out excessive secretions which made her extremely uncomfortable. To watch her suffer made me cringe every time. Yet Laure had to endure this unrelenting routine. I couldn't help but ask God, "Why"? "Why did you allow this to happen to our Laure whose husband and two small kids need her? Are you there? "Yet deep down in my heart, I believed God meant good despite these awful circumstances. I knew I needed to be there with Laure and her family and to go through this ordeal with them.

Several prayer groups were quickly formed to keep round-the-clock prayer vigil. Family and friends came one by one from all over the world

- from the US, London, Taiwan - to be with Laure. Some even brought their spiritual gurus as well as religious objects blessed by their masters in the hopes of healing her. The outpouring of support for Laure was overwhelming.

As the weeks passed, Laure's situation stabilized. Kabir and Laure's dad Paul decided it was time to bring Laure back to their home in California where Laure would have access to the best possible medical care. When Laure arrived back in California, she started a rigorous regiment of physical therapy and acupuncture. A certain

normality of family life returned.

Later, Kabir learned that Rehabilitation Institute of Chicago (RIC), a hospital equipped with state-of-the-art equipment and technology, offered first-class rehabilitation treatment. Soon after, in June 2010, Laure was air-lifted and admitted there. Over the next three months, she went through a grueling regiment of rehabilitation. Laure's dad also found a well-known acupuncturist to treat her. Three months went by quickly. Laure's condition had improved significantly.

Laure returned to the Bay Area in September 2010. Laure's schedule was busier than ever. Not only was she disciplined in her daily therapies, she performed her motherly duties as well. She planned the kids' activities, went to teacher-parent conferences, watched the kids' Christmas plays, celebrated family anniversaries and birthdays. One routine enjoyed by both children and Laure was for Ton Ton and Caillou to sit on his mommy's lap and to be pushed to their school. No matter how bad she slept the previous night, she would always get up to take the kids to school. I loved to see how proud the boys were with their mommy by their side when they were greeted by their teachers. What a beautiful mother-and-sons picture.

Later, Laure told me she went back to work. She kept up with the current political and business news in the world and participated in making key decisions at Asia Alternatives, the company she and her partners founded. In 2013, she was honored in an alumni dinner by her Alma Mater -Harvard University. We were all happy to share her joy.

For the subsequent visits, besides the physical improvements, I began to notice Laure go out more – girls' nights out, dinners with Kabir and friends, listening to seminars, operas and concerts. Occasionally, she invited me to go with her. She was no longer bothered if other people stared at her. She felt confident in herself as much as before. She paid attention to how she looked. She even got her nails painted in different color combinations. When visitors came, she made sure her guests were well cared for. She even consoled her depressed friend. Her focus was shifted from self-pity to caring about other people. In Part 2, Chapter 1 of her book, she said "Most people defined victory (for quadriplegic people) as walking. For me victory meant happiness." She was no longer defined by her disability and happiness was in her grasp. My sister and I said to each other, "Our Laure is back!" Hooray!

Laure's cousin Cherene got married in January 2014. Laure, Kabir and the kids all came to Los Angeles to celebrate our family's happy occasion. She was beautiful in her new hair-do and new gown. We all had a great time. The next day, Laure took the kids to Disneyland. To my amazement, she even rode on all of the most fearful rides I would never have dared to ride even in my younger years. She said, "My whole world opened up and I could see myself doing it all. My victory had just begun."

When Laure's grandma passed away in February 2014, she told us she wanted to come to attend the funeral. My sister and I were very apprehensive. How was she going to get through all the obstacles associated with getting from San Francisco to Los Angeles on a commercial flight? Yet that is what she wanted and I did not persuade her otherwise. Despite a couple of minor glitches, the journey went smoothly. Naturally it was great to see Laure again despite the sad circumstances. Grandma would be smiling in heaven to see that Laure made such a special effort to pay tribute to her at her memorial service.

As I reached the end of her book, my heart was filled with joy, because I began to see where God has led Laure. I recall one time when we were discussing the topic of faith. The story of Abraham in the Old Testament naturally came up. Abraham obeyed God by being willing to sacrifice his beloved son on the altar. At the end, God spared Abraham's son by providing an animal for the sacrifice. Laure began crying. She told me that she was fearful that God would punish her by taking her sons away because she loved her sons more than God. I told her that God would not do that to her. He was not one who delights in seeing human beings suffer. I wasn't sure my answer was satisfactory. Yet I knew she never lost her faith because she knew very well that God has been with her every step of the way in her walk along this difficult path.

Laure has endured what an ordinary person could not endure. One time, I asked myself how it would feel to be in Laure's shoes. I lied in bed trying to be still. I could not bear this even for one minute. Yet Laure has had to endure this hour by hour, day by day, year by year. But it's not the end of the story. If it were, it would have been a real tragedy.

To the contrary, Laure's story is one of courage, hope and triumph. Even during the most seemingly hopeless times, I believe that Laure's determination and tenacity has always been there to propel her through. Every time I went to visit her, she wanted me to watch her physical therapy sessions. She would proudly show me how she could do something she was unable to do before. I would sit on the sidelines cheering her on. We celebrated the slightest improvements knowing full well in the long run they would add up to become bigger milestones in her progress. I saw her being able to lift her head, move her neck, type on the computer via the laser beam from her head light, kick her leg, even stand up on her own, etc.. They were the fruits of Gods' healing as well as her sheer determination.

This past April 26, 2014 marked the fourth anniversary of Laure's tragic stroke. Yes, she has had moments of sadness and frustration, but God has always been there gently reminding her that she is loved. Over the past four years, she has transformed herself into a winning soldier. As she writes in the later chapter of her book "Will," "I lost all fear. And I wasn't afraid anymore because I wanted God's Kingdom and his will." Like Job, Laure has come to terms with God, and she is at peace with Him. As John 16:33 says ".... In the world you will have suffering, but take courage, I have conquered the world." By God's grace and with Laure's husband Kabir's unwavering love and the support of her family and friends, she has come through triumphantly. I am truly blessed to have witnessed her incredible journey so far. As a sermon I heard preached by Rev. Tim Keller proclaims:

· The truly good things can never be taken away.

· God can turn bad things to good.

· The best is yet to come.

I truly believe, for Laure, the best is yet to come!

Reflections on A Changed Life

Last year, Laure told us she wanted to write a book. We all know that when Laure decides to do something to consider it done. I congratulate her for completing this book by her painstakingly spelling out every word, letter by letter. I know so many readers will find courage, purpose and motivation as I do and will be helped by it no matter what circumstances are present in their own lives.

Calvin Wei

I am Laure's cousin on her father's side. I have looked up to Laure for as long as I can remember. Laure has always been the example to me par excellence of beauty, empathy, kindness, intelligence, scholarship, determination and sophistication. Laure's great academic successes were always a given, inspiring us throughout our childhoods; but what was always incredible to me was Laure's preternatural ability to form deep connections with people and to form lifelong friendships with them.

Visiting Laure at whatever stage she was in of her life is always an exercise in being inspired. On visits to her in San Francisco, Hong Kong and Taiwan, I would always wish that I could be more like Laure. Laure is connoisseur of so many things - of places, food, wine, art and literature and she has taught me about what is beautiful in the world. She has always had the most refined and impeccable of tastes: an ardent Francophile, of Domaine Romanée-Conti wines, of Michelin starred restaurants and French cheeses. I love the story that when she visited Alain Passard's restaurant Arpege in Paris that he created special dish just for her with a chorus line of frog legs dancing across her plate.

At the same time, Laure's refined taste is not superficial, but on the

contrary, reflects her tremendous depth of thought and feeling. Laure is gently and generously wise; she has subtly probed and guided me at several critical junctures in my life. She would often recommend books and pieces of music to me which were revealing in ways which were not always easily or directly apparent. Laure and I would often discuss one of our favorite books, "Portrait of the Artist as a Young Man" by James Joyce. The book is ultimately a story of a young artist discovering his vocation and destiny despite all the alienation and troubles of childhood and adolescence. He writes that in the course of life that there are "nets flung at [the self] to hold it back from flight." He proclaims: "I shall try to fly by those nets." This is a fitting description for Laure: despite the obstacles that have confronted her, Laure has soared far and beyond those nets!

I have been lucky enough to share many magical moments with Laure. I remember ever so clearly the morning she and Kabir greeted us at breakfast the day after their wedding day - the bright clean briny air in their faces out on the outdoor terrace at the Princeville hotel in Kauai, her face radiant with happiness. Memories of Laure's wedding in Hawaii always fill me with happiness and nostalgia. Laure in her typical way had arranged it in high, glorious fashion.

I always knew that Laure was going to be an incredible mother. When I visited Laure and Kabir in Hong Kong in January 2010, I had some of the most lovely times of my life. It was the intersection of several magical events: it was Laure's birthday, Ton Ton's fourth birthday and Caillou was just recently born and was enjoying his first weeks at home. Laure had meticulously planned Ton Ton's birthday party complete with a piñata and all of Ton Ton's friends. Just a few days after, we had experienced an exquisite dinner at one of Laure's favorite restaurants in celebration of her birthday. It was an atmosphere of such carefree and contented happiness, the beauty of something tentatively yet gloriously commencing.

When I heard that Laure had a stroke I felt devastated. I felt a tremendous sadness for Laure's suffering, and the impact this would have on Ton Ton, Caillou, Kabir, Laure's father and sister and our whole family. Although events may have diverged from their original path, Laure has been triumphant over her circumstances with her fortitude, determination, courage and ability to love and be loved. Her visit to our cousin Cherene's wedding and our grandmother's memorial service have all proven her tremendous resolve. She is loved by so many and continues to inspire us day by day. Laure has taught all of us to rise above the givens of our circumstances, to expand the reaches of our inner consciousness and continuously to generate deeper and richer possibilities.

Che-Hwa Lee

I am one of Laure's aunts. Laure is our 1st niece in our Wang's family, therefore she is our 1st love from our next generation. She was growing up from a family with loving dad and mom. She was well educated and disciplined from many well-known elementary, middle, and high schools. I constantly heard she performed excellently in school. She went to two famous universities, Stanford University for her undergraduate and Harvard for her MBA. She absorbed both the best of the west and the east cultures of these two different universities.

Laure inherited many good things from her parents. She treats things with discretion and thoroughly takes care of people warmly, and is a very hard worker. Not only she can speak English but also Chinese, Japanese, Latin, and French. During her growing-up period, she stayed in many places because of her dad's business. These abroad experiences made her have a very wide vision. After graduating from Stanford, she worked for Goldman, Sachs & Co. which many new graduates wish they could work for. Later on, she was one of the three young women founders of a new investment company, Asia Alternatives. She was interviewed by one of the reporters from the famous magazine, 今周刊, saying she raised 950 million dollars in funds even at the time of world economic crisis in 2008.

She is a very sophisticated young lady and married to a handsome gentleman, Kabir and loving mom with two lovely boys, Ton Ton and Calliou. We are all so proud of her and very happy for her.

But sad news covered our entire family On Monday, April 26, 2010. Laure collapsed at work and was diagnosed with the most serious stroke. Among these 4 years, we saw Laure climb out from death. We knew there were many excellent doctors whom were searched/requested/begged by her dad and husband to help her. There were also many endless hours by her various therapists and helpers.

There are so much worry, tears, heartbreak from her parents, husband, sister, family members, and friends. I cannot imagine the difficulties, of how much effort to make the nerve and the muscle to reconnect inch by inch.

But with her persistent and her determination, Laure has tremendous improvements as of today.

Laure is working very hard on her busy daily schedules. Certainly our God is with us, and He gave us strength and hope, to go through this difficult time. And Laure did as well as she overcame her difficulties. Although she still has many things in front of her, her spirit is back. She would like to finish her book to encourage people who have a similar situation as her.

Wow! Such a great heart. She does not hide her physical condition

but stands out telling the world she made it and so can they. Her book is not silent but it is shouted.

I thank God and pray that He continuously protects and guides her.

Her parents are so proud of their daughter, Kabir, is so provd of his wife, and Ton Ton and Calliou are so proud of their mom.

Also, we are so proud of our favorite niece.

Uncle and Aunt

Sang and Che-Hwa Lee

Yee Lee

Laure is the cousin in our family that you looked up to. She is well read, highly educated, professionally accomplished, successful in life, sophisticated, and well traveled. Growing up, I would constantly hear about how Laure was doing through my parents. They always pushed me to do as well as her and try to accomplish as much as she had. This made hearing about her stroke and physical therapy all the more devastating. The first time I was told that Laure had a stroke I was shocked. How could that happen to someone that young and seemingly so healthy? It made me immediately reflect upon my life and what was important to me. The stroke happened to be at a critical point in her life and career. A few weeks after hearing about her stroke, I found out that she would be flying to Chicago to receive therapy from Rehabihtation Institute of Chicago, known for treating stroke patients. Being the only cousin in Chicago at the time, I went to visit her and see her for the first time since it happened. I was shocked and scared. It hurt to see the condition that Laure was in. Normally well spoken and always asking how things were with my career and life, all Laure could do was blink and sometimes cry. It hurt to see how helpless she was. I quickly learned that all of us, the family, the nurses, the healthcare providers were there to make sure she retained hope and pushed herself through therapy.

After many months of physical therapy, Laure now lives in the San Francisco area. We go visit her almost once a year. It is good to see that things at home have settled down for her and  she can be with the kids everyday. We hope that she will continue to regain the ability to do activities as she once did without effort. But it is always great to know that she maintains the resolve to constantly improve and will always have the love of her family and friends that support her in her journey.

Laure, we wish you the best and will see you soon. This time we will have baby Sophie in tow.

Love,

Yee, Sharon, and Sophie

Kuei-Mei Liu

Laure, My Oldest Sister's Daughter.

In 1970 my parents asked me if I would like to visit my oldest sister, Susan, because she was pregnant with their first grandchild, Laure. Looking forward to seeing Susan, I left my parents' home in Taipei and came to the US, my first trip to a foreign country. Paul and Susan, pregnant with Laure, picked me up from JFK, and treated me to an eye-opening NYC experience by way of a Radio City movie, Jack Lemmon's "The Out-of-Towners".

During the summer of 1970, Susan's life centered on the tiny Laure inside of her. Susan read books and kept herself healthy. She played classical music, sang and read children's books to Laure. After Paul got home from work, together they would baby talk to Susan's belly. Laure was their love child from day 1.

In 1986 Susan was hospitalized with cancer. I came from Michigan and stayed at her home the first night. Laure came into the guest room, sat on the floor and chatted with me; so mature, gentle, caring and curious at 16.

In 2004 in Princeville of Kauai, during the breakfast get-together after Laure and Kabir's wedding, my husband and I came with the hope of seeing Laure even though we already had our breakfast at the B&B. We sat down watching people feasting on the bountiful spread of food. Laure and Kabir came in, saw us, and asked us to sit next to her. I felt so touched and honored. Even to this day, thinking and writing about it made me teary.

In 2007 Neil and I visited Laure and her family in her beautiful hillside home in Hong Kong. Being a new mother, one of the successful business partners known as "Three Little Dragons" by the Hong Kong society, and with a loving and handsome husband, Kabir, at her side, Laure was radiant, happy and looking forward to new challenges.

In 2010 after Laure was flown from the hospital in Hong Kong to the US, my husband and I followed her family's visitors' schedule, and spent a month with her first in Chicago and then back to California. What a shock to see how ravaged she was physically, emotionally and mentally! Even in devastation, she was able to engage in therapies, discuss business with her partners, listen and respond to caring relatives and friends, and relentlessly work towards her recovery.

Over the past few years, we visited her from Florida and watched, with amazement, her unyielding struggle with determination. During our most recent visit in April of 2014, we carried on the most pleasant and productive conversation about her therapies, the book she was writing, the social occasions she attended, the parenting she took on, the new house designs she worked out with the architect, the business partnership responsibilities she resumed, the birthday gift she planned for Kabir, and her intention of returning to Princeville for her wedding anniversary. With her younger son, Caillou, dozing off at her side and Kabir looking in on her from time to time, as we conversed through her capable staff, Laure was confident, in control and looking forward to new experiences.

Laure, you are an inspiration to us because you are so unbelievably brave and courageous. Your mother would have been so proud of you.

With much love,
Aunt Kuei-mei
July 5, 2014

P. S. Uncle Neil sends his love.

Reflections on A Changed Life

Cynthia Liu

When I was a child, I looked up to my older cousin Laure. I came to the U.S. when I was four, and at that time, Laure seemed so much more American. My aunt Susan, Laure and Joan's mom, made them oatmeal for breakfast-- it was so American and cool. Laure spoke French and could sing Broadway show tunes such as "Tomorrow" from Annie. She wrote me letters from across the country. Though we didn't see each other often, whenever we did, we would talk for hours-- as if we hadn't been apart for long. I spent the summer before I went to college in Taiwan on the "Love Boat" summer exchange program and then stayed with Laure, Joan, and Uncle Paul for a few weeks. Laure always had the funniest stories

and fascinating adventures to share. The entire world seemed to be three degrees of separation from Laure-- she had this gift for knowing everyone. I remember we went to Hong Kong for a few days that summer and while we were there, she ran into an old teacher of hers on the street-- coincidence? No, that was just Laure. And through the years, she has continued to cultivate a global network of movers and shakers. As an introvert, I admire this about Laure-- she just goes out and talks to people, and that is just one among her many talents.

Part Four

Betty Hung

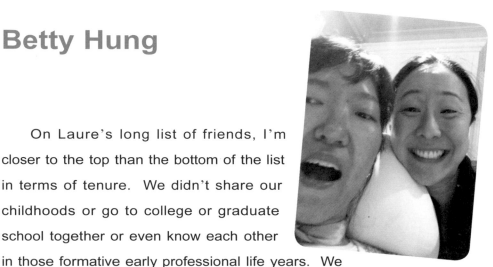

On Laure's long list of friends, I'm closer to the top than the bottom of the list in terms of tenure. We didn't share our childhoods or go to college or graduate school together or even know each other in those formative early professional life years. We met relatively recently, in the late 1990s (yeah, I know that's almost twenty years ago now), which means that compared to Art and Erin and Paul and Jean and Tara and so many others, I'm one of Laure's "new" friends, having met her pretty much at the same time that she met Kabir.

Although our friendship has such a short history, we have managed to accumulate an impressive list of really fabulous and memorable adventures, such as a girls' trip to Thailand, golfing on Lanai, skiing in Park City, our virgin pilgrimage to the French Laundry and countless other gourmet meals. The sheer volume and range of these shared experiences speaks to the quality of Laure's relationships. She not only has more friends than anyone I know, but she also has more "old" friends than any of us and each of her friends, old and new, has an entire album of these kinds of Laure moments that stand out even against the brilliant lives we all lead.

Reflections on A Changed Life

When I first learned of Laure's stroke, I was living in California while she was in Hong Kong. I felt completely devastated by the news and powerless to help her or her family in any way. Given the distance and time differences, we probably hadn't connected in a couple of months and there was the distinct possibility that we would never see each other again. Watching Laure's recovery from when she first arrived in California completely miserable, terrified, depressed and immobile, to her rehab in Santa Clara where they helped her regain her ability to communicate to today where she controls all the important decisions in her own and her family's life, has been one of the most unexpectedly extraordinary experiences. Along the way, we've shared some really special moments that we wouldn't have thought twice about if everything hadn't changed, but today mean more to me than any of those exotic trips or luxurious meals we had in the years prior.

One Saturday, I spent an afternoon with Laure and Ton Ton while she was at Santa Clara. He was just learning (i.e. teaching himself) to read and he patiently sounded out word after word and read stories to her, waiting for Laure to acknowledge each page with a blink before he turned to the next one. It was so precious and intimate that I felt like an eavesdropper.

In the early days after Laure came home, I visited and brought homemade spaghetti and meatballs which I thought the boys might enjoy. When Mely told me that Laure, who was just starting to take solid food, ate an entire meatball, I think I cried.

At the end of a visit once, Laure surprised me with a slow but very clear "BYE..." The whole time I'd been there, we'd been spelling, and I was shocked that her speech had made such progress. It was the first time I had heard her say a word in almost three years. The look of pride and pleasure on Laure's face, for being able to speak so well and, I suspect, for surprising the daylights out of me, was priceless.

In fact, Laure has become very fun and funny. On almost every visit, we've laughed so hard that Laure could hardly breathe, and somehow she always manages to spray me with food, which just makes us laugh even harder. Maybe that is the effect of the "emotional control" thing, but I tell myself that we are truly enjoying ourselves and sharing a moment of pure hilarity. I've laughed harder and happier in the last four years with Laure than with anyone else.

That's not to say that it's been a fairy tale recovery with all sunshine and roses. Seeing Laure struggle through anger, grief, depression, loss has been beyond excruciating, even for me who comes for visits every few months. In the darkest days, which hopefully are well behind us, sometimes there was nothing to be said or done, just to sit.

If you didn't know Laure you wouldn't believe it, but she and I have had the most extraordinary conversations in these last few years. And it's not just because I get to do all the talking either. Laure and I "converse" across a broad range of topics as we always have and she has strong opinions on all of them. She has a new directness and brevity that are quite refreshing. And then if I don't follow her advice, she persists and gives me what I call "stinky blinky eye" which is the equivalent of yelling at me, I guess. When I send her an email and she replies, usually right away, I all but forget that her speech is limited because the words on the page are just Laure's.

There is one big change in Laure that I've seen emerge, especially in the last two years. If you spend time with her, you'll notice it too. She is so present. She is so focused. She sees and hears everything. Gone are the silly superficial distractions we experience every day. She was always such a perfectionist and always trying to please everyone around her. Now she only cares about things that matter to her, her family and her friends and she has freed herself from the expectations of others. It's a good life lesson for all the rest of us.

As Laure constantly reminds me – life is too short. Of course, she is right. And how thankful we all are to still have her in ours...

Chris Warden

I first met Laure in 1995 during our first year of business school. We became fast friends, having both just arrived back from living the expat life in Hong Kong. We found we shared many friends, and bonded over our common experiences as well as our readjustment to being back in the States and back in school.

I have too many stories involving Laure to mention, so I thought I'd focus specifically on our adventures in business school where we were particularly fortunate to spend so many hours and days together. Laure and I love to travel. Our first trip came about in the second semester, when I mentioned how much I wanted to take a break from business school and the dreary Boston weather. Without missing a beat, Laure said she had noticed flights to Paris were going for just $200. I told her about my favorite student-friendly place to stay in the Marais, an area that was still somewhat sketchy 20 years ago. It was a family-run hotel, barely one-step up from a youth hostel, on rue des Mauvais Garcons, which translates to "the street of bad boys". Despite the dubious street name, Laure thought it sounded great. We quickly booked the tickets and had a wonderful time running around Paris in February!

One afternoon I was overcome with jet lag and fell asleep. Laure, who always seemed to be able to fall asleep anytime, anywhere, had naturally slept for the entire flight and was instantly on Paris time. She decided to visit a nearby church, and as she left the church she was surprised by the paparazzi there to photograph a celebrity wedding. They took hundreds of pictures of her exiting the church. Laure never did find out who those photographers were after.

The highlight of our trip to Paris was a very long lunch at l'Arpege. The restaurant was buzzing with excitement, because they had just learned they had been awarded a third Michelin star. As luck would have it, the other diners that day were all staid French businessmen, so we seemed to get some extra attention from the chef. He was intrigued by Laure, and invited us to stay after lunch and join him for a drink and more food at his table. Laure spoke French with him and translated for me. At around 5:00 he gave us a tour of the restaurant, and then

suggested we enjoy some more wine while he went back to work cooking dinner. We continued to enjoy the food and wine at l'Arpege, and finally stumbled out of the restaurant at 9:00 that evening. I have never had a nine-hour lunch before or since!

We also visited Le Grizzli, and ordered the fois gras. Laure and I couldn't decide which wine would be best with the dish. The Frenchwoman sitting next to us insisted we absolutely must order a Sauterne with fois gras. She was upset that we were considering anything else. We followed her instructions so as not to cause a scene and were

Aung Sang Suu Kyi under house arrest before she won the Nobel Peace Prize

very happy to learn about the classic pairing.

The summer after our first year of business school Laure called me and asked if I wanted to join her in Burma for a few weeks before school started again. We made a plan to meet at a hotel in Yangon. Luckily my flight was pretty much on time, and I made it there on the day we had planned, because we had no back-up plan if anything had gone wrong! Somehow we just trusted it wouldn't, and it worked.

At that time Aung San Suu Kyi was under house arrest, but once a week she stood up behind the gate surrounding her home and spoke to a crowd of supporters. We decided to go and hear her. An English-speaking monk who sat next to us translated her speech. Afterwards we asked one of her aids if we might meet her. To our surprise they said we could. We were thrilled to be part of a small group invited to her home to hear more about her struggle for a free Burma. We were amazed by her tireless dedication to the people of Burma and agreed she was the most amazing person we had ever met. We were also probably lucky that Burmese security agents decided we were harmless and allowed us to move around the country without incident. We were young and naïve, and figured we could talk our way out of any trouble if we were questioned.

Our second year of business school we decided the Paris trip needed a repeat. We invited Kerty Nilsson and Kim Rector to join us, and had a wonderful time. Kerty had lived in Paris as a child, and her French came back to her quickly. Laure kept picking up and retaining everything Kerty was saying, and so she seemed to be fluent by the end of the trip. We went back to l'Arpege, and Laure told the chef that she wanted to return to Paris in the summer and learn all about French cooking. She was surprised and thrilled when he offered her an internship at l'Arpege, and she quickly accepted.

Before we left our friend Elizabeth Kuo gave us a present to deliver to her Parisian friend John-Paul. John-Paul turned out to be the maître d' at Guy Savoy, one of the top restaurants in the city, and we were more than happy to combine the present delivery with a decadent eight-course dinner! Laure stayed in touch with John-Paul in the interim, and when she returned to Paris he arranged an internship for her at Guy Savoy. It was very unusual for someone to have internships at two rival three-star restaurants in Paris, but Laure managed to pull it off somehow.

I love Laure's stories about her summer of culinary adventures in Paris. At l'Arpege the chef did not understand that she had no restaurant training at all, so he kept barking orders at her in French and expected her to execute them flawlessly. Laure secretly carried around a French culinary phrasebook, and then looked up the words she did not understand when no one was looking. The chef decided she should be the one to prepare the signature amuse bouche, the "chaud-froid oeuf", which was an egg yolk cooked in the shell and topped with sherry-vinegar infused cream, chives, maple syrup, and salt. Laure needed to cut the tops off of the eggs, and they needed to be perfect. She had no idea how to do it at first, and she destroyed a few dozen eggs in the process of figuring it out. She carefully disposed of the eggs in as many different garbage bins as she could find so the chef would not see how many she had wasted. Eventually Laure did learn how to make the famous dish flawlessly. I think it was the best Parisian souvenir a foodie like Laure could ever hope for.

Over the years I have enjoyed going back to l'Arpege anytime I am in Paris, and of course I have happy memories of all of our adventures that took place there. Laure and I have followed with delight the evolution of the chef's cooking over time as he transitioned to a lighter style with a heavy focus on vegetables. I hope Laure continues to gain strength and movement, and that she can one day make it back to l'Arpege to enjoy another fabulous meal there with friends and family. Keep going my dear friend. I know you can do it.

Elizabeth Spokes

If it weren't for her giant, sway you back and forth hugging, and her constant, disarming giggling, I would have been way too intimidated to hang out with Laure Wang.

We met at HBS where she had a legitimate, stacked CV coming in, yet packed her days with "1"s, singing, acting, speaking multiple languages, PAW dinners (ask Michael Kantrow) and generally dazzling everyone. She was super fun and up for everything.

Our trip to Africa wasn't short of thrills and laughs. As a roommate, Laure told me the most disgusting stories (the one about the most interesting thing you've eaten in China!?). As a travel partner, she conveniently befriended handsome hotel owners and restaurateurs in Zimbabwe and nursed me through a bout of altitude sickness by savoring gourmet meals while I sat next to her, pale and choking down boiled potatoes.

There is a theme of being the friendliest and most adaptable person. As an no-name intern at L'Arpege, Laure stayed out of trouble by darting past big knives and ducking under hot pots as if in a game of Frogger, all while diligently peeling of tomatoes by the crate-load 24/7 for their signature dessert. And the French boyfriend was...wait...did I introduce you two?!

But fair enough, Laure is the most faithful friend. She ultimately connected me to my dear husband through some clever early-day internet thinking! She knew where he worked and figured out what his email might be and voila, "You've Got Mail!"

Laure managed to marry THE coolest guy at HBS, because he wasn't actually at HBS. When Ton Ton was three, we sat in Laure's Atherton garden, both of us pregnant and talking a mile a minute, swaying back and forth with laughs.

Motherhood suits Laure. And her friends benefit from her research and sharp questions, as well as our common bond in now being able to get a word in edge-wise.

It's all good. Close family, two loving boys, two million friends, husband who uncorks bordeaux for girls' lunches, new gadget-packed house, philanthropic work, and now a book! How lucky I am to be in her orbit. What's next Laure?

With love from Elizabeth Spokes
San Francisco,
August 16, 2014

Erin Ganju and Jean Chiang

Friendship. Important of course - and when it is at its best - indispensable and magical. Life transforming. A bond and trust at the deepest level. Being there for one another during the birth of our children and the passing of our parents. The people you want to call first to share news. The person you want the most to be there when you need a shoulder to cry on. When you are with the closest of your friends you are at your rawest. Your true self. No pretense. No judgments.

We've been the best of friends with Laure for over twenty years. It's a friendship that is all of the above and indispensable and magical. The best. We of course have separate memories and stories to share but we almost can't. It's always been the three of us. We all met each other as analysts at Goldman Sachs in 1988 – none of us were in the same department, but we were always in the same restroom. It was our office at 85 Broad - the 20th floor women's restroom. We went there half a dozen times a day - to cry mostly about how tired we were, how overworked we were, to laugh about the latest night out and to plan for our next adventure.

We have stories that make only us laugh. We tell the stories over and over as if they are funny to others but in truth we know. We just like laughing at ourselves. We have memories that no one could possibly

understand but us — a shared history that is ours and ours alone. Our lives are so inextricably woven together that it is hard to remember at times where one of our stories starts and the other's end. (Okay, Erin seems to get the stories mixed up if truth be told, but she sticks by her theory that every good story needs a few embellishments for the listener's enjoyment. Laure of course remembers every detail of every story. Jean denies all, laughs at all - and honestly can't remember what really happened anymore and what we've all made up over time.) We have had fights - terrible ones at times. But we were always speaking our own truth to each other and knew, however bad it would get, we would always return to each other. So we always went straight through

the bad, never around.

But we had no idea what true friendship was until everything we knew was stripped away, and what remained was the depth of Laure's soul staring back at us after she was locked in. We still remember with absolute clarity the calls we received from Kabir sharing what had happened. And the gut wrenching sorrow that followed us the whole plane ride to Hong Kong - is she going to be ok? And will our friendship continue to support and drive us. Would we ever laugh as hard as we always laughed?

Now years later, the answers to all those questions are yes. Laure is not only okay, she is amazing. She has found happiness and a joy and is living for herself as well as her family and friends. She continues to be our rock, our greatest support and listener. And, yes, we laugh and laugh still. And maybe even harder as we realize joy should always be expressed.

Our shared past is a common denominator that brings the three of us together in a laugh or a memory that takes few words to describe. We can finish each other's sentences, we can tell each other's stories. This is essential now that Laure struggles to communicate. It sometimes only takes a word or the description of an outfit and we're all thinking the same thing. The amazing part is that Laure still has the best memory out of the three of us. The fact is that she is exactly the same Laure that we all know and love, but just doesn't have the use of her physical body to express herself in the same way. She still gives advice, listens even more intently at our life's happenings, always goes back to the basic question - "how are you?" And she wants to know all of it.

Laure loves our stories and would like them all retold, but being moms and professionals, there are limits to what we will share in this memoir. Here are some of our PG-13 headliners:

· We laughed, we cried, we bonded over delicious plates of pasta at Carmela's Village Kitchen Trattoria in NY. It was the scene of World War Three, but will always be remembered as "our spot" no matter who else went there (or who else that person brought - like another girl they had also been exclusively dating all summer).

· Saint Lucia was our first trip together. Sleep, sun, sailing (Laure, are you sure you took sailing at Stanford?! Can you get us back to shore?). Turns out she could not. She had failed tacking back to land in that "class." We capsized in St. Lucia, and the resort guys had to come save us. Purposeful? Maybe! We had a new "high" for some of us on that island and learned that we were the best travel buddies ever.

· Bamboo Bernie's – always a crazy night. Irish Pubs never ended well – Jean, are you awake? Nah, she'll be safe sleeping. Just one more beer inside. Laure, why are you hiding under the table, who are you avoiding? And yes it is stupid to hide for a little while only to pop out later. That's awkward. Where do you think he thinks you came from?

· Ever been to a "Linner" – only in New York. And a white dress up vest with a black bra - a must wear outfit if you want to be noticed. Who in this group did that?

· Greece was another great trip. First time we（read: Erin） learned what the World Cup was all about – why was everyone wearing the same yellow football jersey （"We are yellow, we are blue, we are Swedish f#@% you!!）. We bought friendship rings and Erin is still angry no one else wears them. It comes up practically every time we see each other! We stalked a very handsome man named Livio around the island. To our recollection no one got his attention. Laure kept taking a picture of a wine glass against the ocean as we ate dinner at sunset on Mykonos. Over and over. A still object.

· India tested Laure and Erin to the limit. Beetle-nut chewing, crazy driver chasing us through the streets of Delhi coupled with late Monsoon

rains caused Laure to make a dash for the airport early. We could insert the real fight story, but we need another five years before this becomes funny.

· The Sossusvlei Dunes in Namibia to camping in the Okavango Delta (did you know there is a camping toilet brand named "Elegance"?). Our Africa Adventure along with Melissa was the best of the best. Laure could sleep no matter how bumpy the roads were and brought her special workout pants just for the visit to Victoria Falls. Erin, keep it together, just one more small airplane ride. Melissa, no there is no hot water for your shower, and Jean, how many giraffes can you carry home?

· Remember missing your flight to Seattle to visit Erin. Jean and Laure are the only two girls who could talk so much while staring at the plane - they didn't even realize the flight left without them. We had to lie to Erin it say it was mechanical plane issues. I don't think we told her till years later when we were sure her screaming would be minimized.

· Always good times at Laure and Erin's Union Street apartment. The three of us were finally reunited all living in San Francisco. Our Lunar New Year party every year was the best! Laure was always flopping around, tripping over something or screaming and being the life of the party. At one party there was a big crash and somehow Laure ended up half in the fireplace. That's our Laure.

· Laure was a foodie before foodie was a thing. She taught us to order cheese plates for dessert. You know how the best part of the crème brûlée is the burned caramel sugar coating on top? We were eating crème brûlée after a huge steak dinner - Jean convinced us to eat dessert - she's always the one to order dessert. The three of us convinced a waiter to give us a torch and sugar so we could keep making our own top layer. Given our condition, safety was an issue. Wish we had goggles.

· There was the legendary Laure visit to Jean in SF where we went out early and hard - pitchers of Sangrias at Cha Cha Cha's in the Haight. Let's just say Laure made a decision to see the movie "Sense and Sensibility" after many, many pitchers, Jean fell asleep, and then what happened, and next can't be repeated. Not pretty. Not right. On this side of it hilarious. Classic Laure.

· Eventually, we all met our significant others although we will always be life partners of a sort. We would all marry within a year of each other and have our first child all within a month of each other. Life's milestones came in threes. Couldn't have planned it better if we tried. We welcomed guests to the church at Jean and Albert's wedding. Laure sang at Erin and Jeetu's wedding, Jean read a poem. We wore tiny pink bridesmaid dresses at Laure and Kabir's wedding. We all have our own way of doing things, but big moments are not the same unless the three of us are there together.

· We are still creating funny scenes wherever we go. Spa days that don't go as planned, but get us a freebie next time. Aged, home grown pigeon for dinner anyone? Wait if these dishes were carried by a Japanese potter from Japan why does this dish say made in France? Why is Erin dumpster diving for Jean's underwear in a sea of robes?

Friendship. What a deep meaning it has when life is at its simplest. Now more than ever before it means showing up to just be there for each other. Creating more memories and shared good times no matter what twists and turns life takes.

We love you Laure. You are the most wonderful friend. Thank you for sharing so many of your joy list adventures with us. We would not be the same people if we didn't have each other to share our lives with. You encourage and inspire us to live life with grace and joy.

All our love,

Jean & Erin

Fabiola Salvador "LALA"

Unlike most of you guys I did not know Laure before her stroke. I have met many of Laure's friends and family who always have nothing but great things to say about her, her accomplishments and all of the great things she did before she had her accident but I strongly believe she is accomplishing even greater things now. I have worked for Laure for over 3 years now,  and I am beyond honored to have the privilege to work for her and to see firsthand her journey to recovery. To me, Laure has become more than just my boss, she has become my friend and role-model, and as I always let Kabir and her know they are like my second parents. Although I have only known her as a "mute-quadriplegic", she has never let her physical abilities get in the way of accomplishing her goals.

When I first met Laure, she was starting to adjust to her new life. Her boys were very small at the time, and Kabir and Laure hired me as a nanny. I remember when I first started working, I was very overwhelmed with the job. Laure needed constant care, the boys as well, and our staff was very unpredictable. Although my job was being a nanny and helping out with the house work, I also became very hands on with Laure's care because sometimes the nurses wouldn't show up. I learned to spell, transfer, give meds and feed Laure. I had a lot of responsibility, but I felt better about it because I had Laure's guidance. Although Laure can't talk, she constantly spells out to me anything I do wrong and lets me know exactly how she likes things. At first there were many things that we were always doing wrong, so Laure would get very frustrated. After Dibya left in the middle of the night one day, and Mely quit and left the very next day, Berta and Claudia and I were left to take on all of the responsibility of the house. We didn't know at all what we were doing at the time. We were 21 years old and instead of being out partying on weekends, we were living with Laure and trying to help her out the best we could even though we were completely clueless. Laure taught us about eating healthy foods, such as brown rice and whole wheat everything. I even learned about many foods that I never knew even existed. We learned how to make her vitamix, which had many different fruits and vegetables that helped her stay healthy. She spelled to us how she wanted us to take care of her kids. For more than 3 years Laure has helped us with all aspects of the house. Although it is harder for Laure to physically be with her kids 24/7, she still is and has always been in charge of her home. Whenever we have questions, we always ask Laure and she always does her best to help us do things as she normally would.

Even though I help with Laure, most of my day is spent with her kids. I met Caillou before he could speak, and Ton Ton was 4 years old. Ton Ton and Caillou are some of the smartest boys I have ever met, and as they grow up, they always ask questions regarding mommy, which sometimes are hard for me to answer, but only because I feel that I don't want to say the wrong thing. Ton Ton still has many vivid memories of Laure, Kabir, and Hong Kong and treasures them very deeply. He will always tell me Hong Kong stories, and now that he's older, he has opened up more to me and will ask me "When will mom get better?" When Laure's doctors friends come over to the house, he doesn't hesitate to ask if they know when his mom will get better, which of course makes Laure tear up, but he is very understanding with everyone's different answers. As Caillou started getting older he started realizing that his mom was "different" then other moms, as he once told me. Caillou is very outgoing and fearless and has many questions. He will ask Laure to her face, questions such as "Why do you have a wheel chair?" "When can you talk again?", anything that comes to his mind he will ask Laure. Although these questions make Laure tear up, she always spells her best answer, and we always assure both boys that Laure is working very hard towards her recovery, and they are very happy with the answer. As the boys have told me before, "I know my mom works hard I can hear her screaming from her gym". Both boys love doing outings with Laure, such as going to the movies, theme parks, and even simple things like going out for walks. They love sitting on Laure's lap and even fight for whose turn it is to sit on mommy. Not every day goes smoothly at home, and sometimes the boys get upset with mommy as any kid does, but they know that at the end of the day mommy works extra hard for them and loves them no matter what. Before they go to bed, they pray, and they make sure to ask God to help their mom in her recovery. The boys know they are very lucky to still have their mom.

I know Laure considers her LA trip as a turning point in her life, but for me, I think it happened way before that, and I was lucky to be a part of that moment. I remember picking up the mail one day, and there was a letter for Laure from Stanford. It was about her upcoming 20th reunion, and as I read it to her, she was quick to respond and say she wasn't going. She said she hadn't seen many of these people in a while and wasn't ready to go, which was totally understandable at the time. Instead she opted on making a class page and letting everyone know that maybe in the future she would be able to join them at another reunion. About 6 months passed, and we didn't speak about the reunion until friends of Laure's started asking her if they can stay over since she lived so close to Stanford. I remember being in Laure's room when she started to spell: "I want to go to my reunion". I was in shock because I wasn't expecting her to change her mind, especially when she was so set on not going, and the reunion was also just 1 week away. I told her I was very proud of her and happy that she was going because it was going to be a great opportunity for her. She had 3 events to go to, and her friends went with her to all of them. I remember one of the events was her Branner Hall reunion, which she was very excited about because she could see the people she used to live with. Unfortunately on the day of the event, one of the nurses didn't show up to work that day, and Laure was starting to worry that she would not be able to make the event, so she called me to let me know. It was my day off, but I volunteered to go because I knew how important and meaningful this event was for her, and I didn't want her to miss out. I hurried to her house, and I remember packing 4 boxes of Kleenex that day because I thought Laure was going to cry a lot, since she was going to see people she hadn't seen in a long time and explain everything that had been going on, so I knew it would be emotional for her. She made a book with pictures of the boys, and her and Kabir, and a page explaining about what she had been up to since she left Stanford. When we got to the reunion, I showed the book to everyone who came up to Laure to say hello, I have never met someone with as many friends as Laure has. Everyone was excited to see her especially since she had said she wasn't attending. And to my surprise Laure did not cry at all. She was just talking with everyone and they treated her like the "old Laure from Branner Hall", as she said in her own words. I felt like that weekend of the Reunion changed Laures attitude towards adjusting to her new life and it showed her that she's still the same outgoing person she always was.

Meeting Laure and being welcomed by her family has been a life changing experience. I know my attitude towards life has changed in a positive way thanks to her. I have seen her for over 2 years trying to write this book and get her story out there for her to share with all of you. I have seen her cry because the Dynavox was frustrating her even though she is just trying to type a simple chapter. I have seen her feel like a weight lifted off her shoulders after her eyes finished writing certain chapters and being able to get her thoughts heard. Her perseverance is amazing, and I am grateful and honored she has asked me for the past 2 years to make sure her book is safe and being shared with all of you. Because of Laure, I have learned to never give up no matter the circumstance. I have seen Laure go from asking why this terrible thing happened to her, to her being happy to be alive. She has taught me to never lose faith and always believe that God has a plan for you even though at times you might not think so. She has taught me to be a great friend, even though you might not be doing well yourself. She is always thinking of others, even though she knows she still has her own journey to recovery. When her friends or family need help she always stays in constant contact to make sure they are doing okay and even offers to help make meals when they cant. I will always treasure the time that she and Kabir held a private room dinner for me and my husband with all of the staff at Left Bank because they knew we had a very small ceremony and not a lot of money at the time. Both Kabir and Laure go out of their way to help others and given their situation, it would be understandable if they only focused on themselves, but they don't. That is something that I too want to make sure I do, I want to make sure to help others no matter what I'm going through in life. Laure has taught me how to be a great friend, a great wife and hopefully one day I can become as great of a mother as she is.

Thanks Laure for everything you do.

Frances H Mikuriya, PhD
(Frances Chan)

My memories of Laure date back to high school in Taipei. Although Laure moved back to the US after a year in Taiwan, I still have vivid memories of the times we shared when we were fourteen. I think anyone who knows Laure would agree that the moments with her are usually unforgettable. Laure carries a certain kind of magical effect. She is someone who has a special spark in her personality. If she walks into any place at any time, she can easily transform the atmosphere from gloominess to happiness, boredom to excitement, and anger to laughter.

Laure came to join us in ninth grade at Taipei American School when her family relocated from New York to Taipei. Although Laure was Chinese, she was more like an American expat, she could barely speak a word of Chinese. This didn't really matter since everything was taught in English at our school. However, it didn't stop Laure from wanting to improve her Mandarin. Since Laure was definitely not a shy person, she practiced speaking Chinese at every opportunity she had, conversing with anyone - the cab driver, the department store sales agent, or any random stranger on the street (which often worried me!). When she made mistakes with the language, there was no embarrassment for Laure - we just laughed it off! Her passion to learn and her curiosity are

perhaps some of the many reasons why she is so fun to be with; she has the ability to connect with anyone despite the generation gap, the difference in culture and background. Laure is a rare individual. She is at the same time highly intelligent and a high achiever; she excelled in everything she was involved in, from academia（Stanford and Harvard） to her career, which sky-rocketed, yet she has none of the arrogance that too often becomes the defining trait of many successful people. Laure is surprisingly modest. Everyone felt comfortable with Laure.

I am so grateful that our paths crossed nearly 30 years ago. Although we haven't been in touch consistently and lived in different cities（I moved around a lot and relocated to London in 2002 to pursue my doctorate studies in architecture), Laure is a friend for life. Many friendships dissipate or terminate; with Laure distance does not affect friendships. During the last 30 years, every time we have met up, we have had endless conversations and laughed continuously - we had bonded like we had never been apart. Despite not having seen each other for years, Laure was always the same Laure, so full of passion and excitement for life, with an abundance of love for others, especially her family and friends.

In 2004, I went to Laure and Kabir's wedding in Kauai, Hawaii; I had the honour of being one of the bridesmaids. From my previous experience as bridesmaid to several of my girlfriends, I have learned to anticipate quite a high level of stress involved in the entire occasion. Laure was by far the most fun and laid-back bride to be. This was not surprising at all, since Laure has always looked after others for as long as I have known her. Her wedding was a celebration for her marriage to Kabir, but it was also important for Laure that it was a celebration for family and friends to get together from all over the world - she made sure that everyone would have a good time, and everyone sure had a blast.

In 2008, Laure came to London on a business trip from Hong Kong. Staying only for a couple of nights, her schedule was extremely hectic and packed with meetings. Although she was exhausted, I knew that she would make every effort to find time to catch up with her old friend, even if this would mean sacrificing her rest and sleep. Once again, we caught up like the good old days. Except this time, she had even more stories to tell me. Her face lit up as she was telling me all about her baby son, Ton Ton who at the time had just turned 2 years old. Laure looked the most radiant that I have ever seen her, despite the fact that she had just flown in on a long haul flight on the same day. Wow, I was thinking, what an amazing mother Laure is; her capacity to love is just incredible. Her work is highly demanding, yet she can still find the balance between work and family. I admired her even more than before.

In 2010, I heard the most devastating news from our mutual high school friend Shirley that Laure had a stroke in Hong Kong. When I heard the news, I was looking at a card that Laure had recently sent me from Hong Kong, which I had placed in front of my desk. It was a beautiful family picture of her, Kabir, Ton Ton and the newborn baby Caillou, taken by her sister Joan. I was in disbelief to hear that Laure had suffered a stroke. Shirley went to see Laure and kept me posted on Laure's situation. When Laure was transferred to a hospital in Stanford, our friend Patrick kept me updated. I knew I had to go and see Laure. I wanted to give her as much support as I possibly could, and I knew every bit mattered at this fragile moment. I got in touch with Kabir and Uncle Paul and made a trip from London to visit her in June, not long after she was transferred to the hospital in Stanford. At the time, Laure was frail; in fact she was extremely frail. I knew her frailty was only in her physical body, but mentally she was strong because she had always been a warrior with the strength to overcome any adversity. But then

again, how am I supposed to know? I have read that some locked-in syndrome sufferers have given up on life because life had become unbearable. I could not relate to how much Laure was suffering; no one could relate to the pain she must have been undergoing. We could only pray for her to get better and for her to be hopeful.

I stayed at Laure and Kabir's home in Atherton for 5 days and went to see Laure daily. All I could do as a friend was to be there. I asked Uncle Paul and Kabir whether I could help while I was there. There wasn't much I could do. Everything was organised, and there was never a single moment when Laure was not surrounded by her family or friends. I was very touched to see the amount of support Laure had. Kabir, Uncle Paul, and her Aunt Sylvia did not rest - they were fighting for Laure's recovery as if they were fighting for their own survival. I heard that Joan (who I had missed when I was there) was constantly by her sister's side. There was even a rotating shift schedule for her friends to visit Laure. And this list was always full. The love I witnessed towards Laure was incredible.

One day while I was staying at their home in Atherton, I was asked to give the two boys and the nannies a ride to the hospital. The minute Laure saw her children, tears rolled down her cheeks; her emotions were uncontrollable. My heart ached, and I had to hide my own tears. My memories flashed back to dinner in London just two and a half years ago when she was such a proud mom telling me stories of Ton Ton. I knew that for the love of her children, husband and family, she would persevere and overcome her illness. I went back to London confident that Laure's health would improve. She would fight to get better and would overcome any obstacles and difficulties she had to face.

When I received an email about Laure's book, I was thrilled. Laure is the same old Laure, capable of making anything which seems impossible possible.

Jean Chang

"Friend of Bride"

I had the privilege of reading at Kabir & Laure's wedding (well, one of their weddings – the one on Kauai), and it's funny that their wedding program listed me as "Friend of Bride" because at that point, I thought I was friend of groom. I knew Kabir first (we worked together at Morgan Stanley our first jobs out of college), but now almost 10 years later, I think that wedding program was quite prescient!

It started with our honeymoon. I was lucky enough to attend also their wedding reception in Calcutta. While Kabir had to hurry back to work, Laure and I were able to spend more time traveling around India. I like to joke that I got to honeymoon with Laure and she was lucky to have me given that Kabir had proven to be a terrible tourist – in his home city, he had never been to Coffee House and tried to discourage us from using rickshaws! Laure and I had enormous fun seeing some of the famous Indian highlights – our driver Raju took very good care of us (although Laure had some moments of squeaking in terror from the back seat as he aggressively passed some road obstacles), a very romantic hotel in Udaipur tossed rose petals in our path, we rode camels into sand dunes, and met Charles & Diana look-a-likes at a tea estate in Darjeeling. We spent 24/7 together and talked non-stop (I'm sure

Raju was grateful for the few moments of silence in the backseat when we would share the earbuds of her iPod), and I got to know Laure much better.

I now see myself as definitely "Friend of Bride." Since the stroke, those qualities I admire in Laure have stayed true. Her love of friends and family keep her going. She's wicked smart and almost scarily

determined. She's curious and thirsts for updates not only on what's going on outside but also inside with those around her. I'm really glad that she writes in her book that she has realized that she can't wait to be happy and that happiness has to be in the present — it's so true and I hope she realizes that her happiness brings joy to so many of us.

Joel Wagonfeld

Amazing. That's the one word I would use to describe Laure: not only before, but also – and even more so – after her life-changing stroke.

Other words – such as brilliant, empathetic, hilarious, loving, loyal, generous, gregarious, FUN, deep, insightful, inspirational … and many others – that I might have used to describe Laure prior to her stroke are ones I would use even more emphatically now. I have had the honor of witnessing how Laure has dealt with this extreme adversity by focusing and executing – in her patient, methodical way – on doing the HARD work – day in and day out – that's been necessary for small steps of progress, which have cumulatively resulted in significant progress. Seeing her determination and grit, often juxtaposed with moments of great happiness (uncontrollable laughter) or sadness (inconsolable grief) has intensified my respect, and admiration for Laure, which was already significant.

I continue to treasure her friendship, which has always been unique to me, but now it is unique in an even deeper way. While I wish I could have been there more for her, I continue to be amazed and surprised – every time I am with her – not only by her progress; but also her friendliness, helpfulness, understanding, compassion, sense of humor,

positive outlook, selflessness and wisdom. Just one example: as only Laure could do, she has managed to remain in control of a number of complex factors — such as her family (she rules the house with an iron fist), a huge construction project, re-engaging with the firm she co-founded, constant physical rehabilitation, and — perhaps most challenging, in my mind: the process of coming to terms with what has happened to her, and to paraphrase her own words, finding a positive reason to live; a desire to create happy memories; and a sense of thankfulness for the many things she has not lost (rather than focusing only on the setbacks that she will have to work incredibly hard to overcome).

I met Laure in 1988 at Branner, our freshman dorm at Stanford. While I don't recall the details of how exactly we first connected, I'm pretty sure I met her early on and we were soon "study buddies". I say

I'm pretty confident about this because although I don't have a great memory, there are two things about Laure that stick out in my mind from those early days in Branner when we first bonded as study-buddies.

First: Our study-buddy time was quite limited, since we had very little overlap in classes other than the mandatory Great Works, a class on key literary works that was required for all freshman students.

That's primarily because we had no other classes in common. Laure was taking things' like Japanese, advanced Mandarin (which she already spoke), Advanced Calculus, Physics, Quantum Mechanics and who knows what else … while I was taking full advantage of Stanford's Liberal Arts education via classes such as Intro to Sociology, Intro to Psychology, Windsurfing and Intro to Human Sexuality (one of the most popular classes on campus, believe it or not).

Second: While I came to Stanford with pretty good confidence – having turned down Harvard, and knowing Stanford was the toughest school to get into – statistically speaking – that year, I also expected to encounter some great intellects. However, I never expected that my smartness bubble would be burst by one of the funniest, goofiest (see "Spaz" episode below), caring people I would yet have met … Laure.

She was one of the first people I would randomly meet and agree to study with, and she would also turn out to be one of the smartest people I had yet encountered. Not only was she REALLY smart, but also funny, outgoing, attractive and really organized. For example, during one of our early study sessions, I decided I'd get a bit ahead of the game and jot a few notes about my thoughts regarding the assigned reading for our next class. So, when our study session came around the night before, Laure shows up with a four page typed summary of the assigned material, complete with her own commentary, references and questions. I was so embarrassed I don't think I even pulled out my one page of handwritten chicken scratch.

That's not to say she didn't have her awkward moments. I think I can lay claim to coining her nickname, "Spaz", through much of freshman year, as the result of a situation in our dorm cafeteria. I frankly don't recall whether I quietly snuck up on her to startle her or she simply lost her balance or she tripped (all equally possible in my view). But, what ensued was a circus-quality spectacle, featuring Laure as a weeble-wobbling freshman, making lots of noise and simultaneously trying to balance a full tray of liquids and messy food ... utterly to no avail. Both Laure and the tray (and of course all of its contents) ended flying up in the air and then, as if in slow motion, landing on the floor — right in the center of a room with 100+ other freshman (whom she was still trying to get to know) staring at this zany woman. Unlike many of us in the room, Laure took it in stride, laughing harder than anyone else in the room and good-naturedly fielding the comments from the peanut gallery. It was at that point or sometime shortly thereafter that I dubbed her "Spaz", because of the way she had reacted to the initial loss of balance. And for whatever reason, other situations seemed to back up that nickname ... so, combined with Laure's good nature and her ability to laugh at herself, it stuck.

Life with Laure as a friend, confidante and dorm-mate was full of so many entertaining stories that they could fill pages. But there are a few that strike me most readily, either for their sheer humor or how they reflect the poignancy and importance we have each played in each other's lives:

Laure turns 21:

I'm not sure how I ended up taking Laure out to celebrate on her 21st birthday, because Laure was probably the most popular friend I had on campus. EVERYBODY knew Laure and everyone loved her. But somehow I got the honor of taking her to the OLD Miyake's – quite literally a hole in the wall on University Avenue – to celebrate her 21st birthday. Perhaps her actual birthday fell on a bad night, or perhaps I was just one of many celebrations that she was having that week (in retrospect, I imagine it was the latter). Anyway, to make a very long night/story short, highlights included:

· Laure doing a few warm-up sake shots while characteristically standing on top of her chair;

· Laure successfully downing an entire "Birthday Bowl", which consisted of three bowls of sake, each of which got increasingly large, from a soup bowl until a 12-inch platter;

· Laure puking in my powder-blue Ford Tempo (not surprisingly, but this was decades before Uber); and

· Laure, after assuring me she was fine to stand on her own (and me foolishly believing her) bumped the wall of her dorm so hard that she left a small dent (which is probably there to this day).

Joel helps Laure with an emotional crisis/decision (I think)

This is one of the few times that I can think of when I may have "paid forward" some of the help and consolation that Laure has provided for me – even while she has been dealing with her own adversity (for which I feel guilty). But all I can say (and truly remember) about this was that Laure was in a relationship that was going toward a level of commitment that she did not think she was ready for, or at the very least was not sure she felt comfortable (or honest) representing as being her feelings – yet she was very stressed out and concerned about what to do, how to discuss it with her family and the other person, whether to just go ahead, etc.. In short, it was one of the few times I've ever seen Laure uncertain of herself or a decision – but I did sense that she was fairly certain that she felt ambivalent about it.

So, at least the way I remember that period, we spent many late nights on the phone talking about it, trying to figure out what she really did and didn't feel; who she really was trying to please (or avoid upsetting); etc.. I remember sitting on the fire escape of my apartment in San Francisco – I don't recall where Laure was living at the time. In hindsight I believe Laure made the courageous and COMPLETELY right decision – i.e., while I like to think I helped her through it and facilitated her ability to come to the decision with conviction, let's face it – in the end Laure would probably always make the right decision, even if she has no one else to bounce things off on.

Laure helps Joel with an emotional crisis/decision

Laure has been there for me so many times that I can't even count – including quite literally almost every time I go to see her or be with her since her stroke. This capacity for selflessness and caring – and her ability to inspire and instill others with positivity even as she faces indescribably hard challenges on a day to day basis – is one of the reasons my admiration, love, concern and respect for Laure has grown even stronger and bigger than it ever had been before (which was already way more than for most other people I've ever had in my life).

In short, ever since I first met Laure over 26 years ago, I've realized she is an incredibly amazing and unique individual who I hoped would be in my life for many years to come. The events that have transpired since then – and the ways that she has dealt with them – have only deepened my respect, admiration and caring for her. I truly consider it an honor to call Laure a close friend, and I hope to continue to learn from and be amazed/inspired by her (and perhaps even teach her a thing or two every once in a while) for many years to come.

Love you Laure – the world is a better place because of you!

Reflections on A Changed Life

Julie Cho

I still remember the first day I met Laure. It was freshman year at Stanford and I was at my first fraternity party. I didn't know what to expect, but it turned out to be a mild mannered affair of let's say "good, clean, fun." I met a lot of new and interesting people that evening, but I distinctly remember Laure making a big impression. She was so friendly and beautiful, but above all, incredibly charming. She had a megawatt smile and was so fun to talk with; I looked forward to seeing her again.

Although we didn't have any classes together and we pledged different sororities, our friendship grew steadily each year as we had many friends in common and found ourselves at the same social events. Soon, Laure, Amy, Verna and I became known as the "Asian Invasion" as we showed up places together ready to get things started. Everyone who knew Laure loved her. She was a joy to be around, told the best stories and was so easy to talk with. Her charisma, sense of humor and warmth were lost on no one.

Laure and I also managed to have some fun going through job interviews with some of the same firms during senior year. One time, we were both flying to LA for final rounds and decided to have Super Shuttle drive us to the airport early in the morning. There we were, waiting on the curb in our matching crisp white blouses, conservative

black suits and floral scarves with roller bags and organizers in hand. Halfway to the airport, the driver asked us which airline we worked for. We just looked at each other and burst into laughter. We still don't know how many flight attendants he's picked up from the Stanford campus at 6:00 in the morning. For sure, we shared many laughs, adventures and good times during college.

The summer before Laure entered HBS, I had the good fortune of spending time with her in Hong Kong. In contrast to our college days when we all ran around in packs, we had more opportunities to get together one-on-one and got to know each other even better. Inside this incredibly fun-loving, ambitious and polished young woman was a very thoughtful and sensitive soul who cared deeply about her family and friends. Even though her plate was very full, she was always thinking of others and what made them happy. I was especially touched whenever she talked about her father or sister. She was fiercely determined, strong and brave yet delicate and vulnerable at the same time. In essence, she was a study in contrasts, the very thing that makes one so lovable and real.

Since then, Laure and I have traveled a bit in Southeast Asia together, overlapped a semester at HBS, been a part of each other's weddings and had numerous meals together whenever we were in the same city. All manner of interesting and enlightening conversation awaited us when we got together and I have always enjoyed her company so much. Even though busy schedules, distance and life

circumstances have made our meetings less frequent, I have always held her friendship dear.

As we have seen Laure work so hard the last few years, our love and admiration for her only grows.   For only someone with her character and her love for life, family and friends could endure the hardships and dark moments that she has to emerge with newfound energy, perspective and wisdom to build a fulfilling life with as many joys as can fit in each day. She is blessed to have Kabir, Ton Ton and Calliou, her family and friends, and no one could be more deserving of this unconditional love.

Quite simply, Laure is amazing and I can only hope that she knows how much people think of her and how much love is being shined upon her from every corner of this world.

Kyung Kim

My friendship with Laure has three facets. She is a friend, an advisor on my personal board and family. There are numerous memories that tell the story of building this 3 faceted friendship. Many of them get recounted and relived with Laure's caregivers who are learning more about her through the voices of her friends. Laure has said to me several times that she has many acquaintances, knows a lot of people, but liked having fewer close friends. A view I share. Looking around, I see this is very true as many of her friends have been in her life for multiple years, some decades going back to days of flash dance curls and shoulder pads or even further back into adolescence. This was first made evident at her wedding weekend in Kauai.... where I missed the wedding.

Laure and Kabir's wedding was a large reunion for many guests, and there we discovered how our lives had a common connector in Laure and, or Kabir. Many of us had been friends with each separately. It was unclear for some (despite Kabir's petitioning) where they should sit - on the groom side or bride side. Some had been friends since childhood, high school, college, business school, and many friendships were forged through a common experience in investment banking when it used to be a cool job. It was a grand weekend of reconnecting and

159

celebrating life as two friends decided to share one together.   There is a vivid memory of a very svelte Laure, smiling without a care in the world, swimming, drinking and laughing with us. We owned the pool at Princeville. Laure was a very happy bride.

On the day of the wedding a group of us took a surfing lesson in the morning. Yes, a bad idea. The lesson actually went superbly until it all went awry when a clumsy accident left me writhing in pain. Model-esque life guards came to my rescue, while perfectly coiffed ambulance doctors in sunglasses assessed my condition on this perfectly white sand beach. A scene out of Baywatch if it weren't for the fact I was the one broken and exposed.

It was agreed this incident should be kept hidden from the bride, at least for the night. At the wedding stealth collaborators covered up my accident.   Already there had been a mishap on the beach when Steve Lin had stepped on a sea urchin and was left hobbling around with a hobbit like foot. He refused all offers of the bio remedy for sea urchin stings. Friends snatched away my name tag, made up excuses why I was not to be seen from being in the bathroom to being too busy doing shots with old friends. Upset that I had not come up to congratulate her throughout the night, Laure finally demanded an explanation, and then the secret was out.

A very beautiful but drunk princess bride showed up to my room where I lay with a sling-ed broken clavicle. Sand was still full in my hair even after friends and not nearly close enough girl friends of friends tried to wash and clean me up. A humbling experience needing the assistance of people to help me shower. So, there was the new Mrs. Misra who at the foot of my bed was in tears for her friend who barely could move due to the pain and psychedelic effects of Vicodin. I felt horrible in more ways than one and Laure knew it. She tried to console me and make me feel better on HER wedding day. "Like a bird you have broken your wing". Collapse - brief silence as she passed out. Then a few seconds later in the midst of recounting of my accident, she awoke "......like a bird.. a little bird...your wing is broken...." Then down again for the count. This repeated a couple of more times until finally Kabir carried her away with an emergency garbage pail in hand. It got filled soon after.

I first met Laure many years ago in 1996 during the final year of the wild, wild west days of pre-97 handover in Hong Kong. I recall in one of our first encounters Laure and I bonded over having mutual friends like Charlotte Kuo, one of my few Taiwanese friends, who was a classmate in Japanese school when I was living in Tokyo after college.   Around the same time in 1995, I also first met Kabir as a colleague at Morgan Stanley. Kabir worked in the US but came to visit our mutual friend, John Myers, who worked in the same Hong Kong office. Interesting to look back and see how these two seemingly different people would marry and build a family. Anyone who knew Kabir pre-Laure would know that he has gone through a bit of boot camp for time management and developed a high palette for fine food and wine as the new wine cellar and frequent cravings for foie gras, duck confit and epoisses can attest. And for those who knew Laure pre-Kabir may agree that he taught her to have a more carefree attitude and gave her a new found appreciation for discounts. Before electronic groupons there was Kabir's coupon book.

Although Laure and I have known each other for double digit years, our friendship deepened after her engagement to Kabir and the other facets of our friendship bloomed. In 2002, I was living in NY when all of a sudden I got a call from Kabir. He was in the Bowery. There are only a few reasons to go down to the Bowery and since I knew Kabir was not in the market for restaurant grade kitchen goods or lamps, there was only one answer why a young Indian investment banker would be down there – he was shopping for diamonds. He asked if I would like to see the diamond he was considering for Laure's engagement ring. The phone barely left my ear before I jumped in a cab downtown.

A woman in a diamond shop could be a dangerous combination. Kabir showed me his choice -a beautiful emerald cut diamond of respectable carat size and all the right other "C"s. I felt it was my duty as Laure's girl friend to make sure the diamond fit the girl wearing it. I felt it was my duty as Kabir's female friend to make sure a man in a diamond shop got it right. Kabir did good. I was nearly brought to tears thinking of how happy Laure would be seeing her ring. But before I could give the thumbs up I was nearly blinded by this beacon in the showcase. "Wait. What about this one Kabir? Laure is not a smallish

Asian girl so you may need something bigger. After all, you'll only get married once…." That is all the savvy sales person needed to hear before the baton was passed and he went for the kill. "Oh sir, your friend has fine taste…" he started…. Yadi-yadi-yada, Laure's ring got a carat upgrade, and Ronti had to write a larger check as a bridge loan to seal the deal. To this story, I will add that there was actually a larger 4 carat yellow canary diamond that I also had my sights on. Sorry, Laure. You're welcome, Kabir …

From that moment of having had a small part in Laure's engagement to Kabir, our friendship evolved, and Laure became an advisor on my personal board. She is a valuable confidant, having given me her ear to help me think through important decisions from time to time. This aspect of our friendship still thrives as we talk each time I visit her in Atherton. As an advisor, she was one of the supporting voices to convince me to move to Tokyo to work for Shinsei Bank. It was going to be a big career changing move – to set up a de novo alternatives program and build an investment team from nothing with a new boss living alone in Tokyo. It was a lot to take on in one job change. She encouraged me to go for it - take on the challenge. With She and Kabir in Hong Kong we could be closer together all living in Asia.

I was able to reciprocate in giving Laure some advice later on in one of my Hong Kong trips. We sat on the couch in Branksome on Tregunter Path as Laure revealed to me that she was contemplating parting ways with her dad to start a new career on her own. She would

become a founding partner of a new Asia dedicated private equity investment firm with two friends she had known for years. Since I was working as a LP for Shinsei Bank, the idea that we could potentially find ways to collaborate and work together was very exciting. After much discussion my advice was to go for it - take the risk and reap the upside of your independent success which was in near sight if she wanted it. The rest, as one says, is history, and I became one of her first LPs in Asia Alternatives.

At some point during the years of sharing life, work and play in Asia, our friendship evolved further and Laure became a kind of sister I never had. This may sound odd since I actually have two sisters whom I love dearly but differently. Biology does not always dictate being best friends with your siblings and sometimes we cannot fully relate to our siblings varying life choices. If you are lucky, some people you meet along the walk of life can become sisters and brothers not by birth but by choice. Laure is such a sister.

Laure and Kabir and then Ton Ton, Caillou with the extension of Mely and Dibya became a part of my unconventional Asia family away from my NY home of Korean parents and sisters. Those who have had the experience of an expatriate life may understand that living abroad comes with it excitement and independence, but also some loneliness as you miss holidays, vacations and simple day to day living with family. So, you create a different kind of home and family among friends to stay grounded. Such was the case with my Chindian family in Hong Kong. I enjoyed celebrating Ton Ton and Caillou coming into this world, taking vacations together in Thailand and Bali and sharing quite a few home meals (as well as some coupon dinners out) together. Although I think I may have often been mistaken for a fair skinned (high end) nanny on some of our vacations the memories of these travels are very precious in my own book of life.

In Hong Kong, I was often the auntie who stayed the weekend, said goodnight to the rest of the family as they got ready for bed at 9pm and then went out like the young adult still living under the parents' roof. I was also able to be the auntie that shared some fond memories of the kids growing up. Ton Ton's first birthday was one of them. The day started with presents. Ton Ton loved taking pictures so he got Laure's old Olympus. He was overjoyed when he played with this used camera which in his eyes was the best thing ever. Then we had a fabulous seafood feast in Aberdeen with Laure's dad (Ton Ton's YeYe) that progressed to the idea of giving Ton Ton several finger sips of sauterne (a discerning palette was developed early). Unfortunately this ended with Ton Ton's first hangover experience.

There were also some funny modern family moments. Once, during Caillou's first week we all gathered in the living room awaiting a special visitor. Sitting with Laure, Laure's dad, Kabir (watching golf probably), Ton Ton (playing with Dibya), Caillou (passed out waiting for his next feeding) and Mely (in the kitchen fixing up next batch of pork bone soup - one of Laure's favorites), the unusual visitor arrived. Laure hired a lactation specialist who brought with her an unconventional device to stimulate the milk ducts to get working (another story better told in person, perhaps not appropriate for documentation into something that may wind up as a coffee book).

So, as a friend, advisor, and a sister of sorts, the day in April 2010 happened. I got another call from Kabir. It was not a bad dream. Laure was in the hospital. I got on a flight thinking I would be going to say my goodbye. The months that followed afterwards are in many ways a blur. It is like I was on auto pilot. Something I only used to experience after late nights of drinking. Without taking note, I would get myself home, face washed, teeth brushed, in pajamas with a bottle of water next to my bed without clear memory of how I got there.

I had just left Shinsei so taking time off to stay in Hong Kong was like fate. I wanted to be there and help. But, I often wondered how and where could I contribute. I was not a connected person in Hong Kong. My medical knowledge did not go beyond being premed at university. I had no parenting experience and could not even drive. So, I just went to Hong Kong to be there. Sometimes this was literally just being present, sitting in silence accompanying Kabir and the nannies to the hospital. I met so many people through this time and the outpouring of love from family and friends was quite astounding. An envious wealth of love surrounded Laure during the early period after her stroke at Queen Mary in Pok Fu Lam.

Once Laure had been moved to the US, there was a big exhale in the hopes that she would get better care. While Kabir and her family sat by Laure's side, I was asked to accompany the kids and bring them over from Hong Kong. Although I am a US citizen as are the kids with passports (something Laure had miraculously just sorted out before her stroke), I still feared that I would be interrogated by the immigration officer and at worst detained. I, an unmarried woman, was flying in from Asia with two young ones (one a newborn) in tow and a Nepalese nanny to boot. There were nervous thoughts of how bad this could appear to suspicious minds at immigration.

The journey was kind of a masquerade as Dibya and I tried to make Ton Ton feel like it was a big treat, an adventure to travel without mom and dad. We sat in business class seats (thanks to Laure's dad), had bubble water in the airport lounge and introduced Ton Ton to coke (although it may not have been his real first given who his Baba is). We took pictures of our trip and laughed a lot as we tried to fill Ton Ton's head with all the great things he could look forward to in his new home in the bay area. But when the kids were asleep, in silence I know Dibya and I shared similar pangs of uncertainty and solemn thoughts in facing the reality of why this trip was happening. One day when he is older, I will ask Ton Ton whether he remembers this journey home.

Now after the stroke, our friendship is evolving. Although I still live in Tokyo, Laure and I are able to spend time 2-4 times a year when I visit the bay area. In many ways nothing has changed. Her snapchats, text messages and occasional facetime calls are small reminders of that. It feels good when I am able to know the rest of the sentence she is spelling out without her having to say all the words. There's frustration when the conversation is out of sync. There have been adjustments, of course, many of which she has led in helping me to adopt and fit into in the new now. She has accepted what has happened, unhindered by her condition and resolved to never give up. Knowing Laure, she will continue to surprise in her development, and I look forward to being there as we near 20 years as friends.

Reflections on A Changed Life

Linda Wu

I believe that there are many good people in this world. However, Laure is special. She is not just a good person but one with a heart of gold and an inspiration to us all – both well before and after her stroke.

To me, Laure is the perfect woman and still is. With her pure intelligence, unfaltering capabilities and steadfast stamina – we all know that she excelled academically and professionally. Her achievements are certainly no easy accomplishments but more importantly, she has done so with honor and integrity, which I admire above all.

I know Kabir from our formative years working together and by choosing Kabir as her husband and soul mate, Laure chose kindness, wisdom and compassion. Laure and Kabir have brought to this world two precious boys who magnify their brilliance and charm. I always see Laure's eyes glow with love and pride for her boys.

Laure is full of love and compassion for her friends. She is always there for us, with insightful advice and support. Around a day or two before her stroke, Laure emailed me to see how I was doing as she knew that I was going through a rough patch. This is Laure – she has so many things going on but she always remembers you.

I am always thinking of Laure too. She is my inspiration to do the best that I can. She is also my inspiration to be brave in the face

of adversity. I don't know why bad things happen, especially to good people, but when it does, we must remember to muster up Laure-like strength and perseverance.

I love reading Laure's manuscript as I can finally hear her words. Laure showed us that we don't need many words to express ourselves and evoke emotions. This is one of her many gifts to us, her words will touch so many people. When I was last visiting Laure, I talked and talked and she asked a few questions and made some comments. With just those succinct remarks, she gave me fresh ideas. That's Laure's insightfulness.

Putting together this contribution to Laure's book also reminded me how important it is to take photos and commemorate our friendships. I've always been the lazy one with photographs, relying on family and friends to make the effort. To my disappointment, I could not find any photos of Laure and me together. Refusing to accept this, I asked my friendly photographer to digitally adjust photos from my wedding in 2005 – from which I do have photos of Laure – so that we have a photo together. This photo is special as Laure was pregnant with Ton Ton then.

While we will have more opportunities to do so, I do wish that we took many more everyday photos together. A photo of when we were sitting at the patio of Ladies Recreation Club in Hong Kong, just chatting about family, friends and life on a beautiful, sunny afternoon. A photo of one of my visits to Laure and Kabir's home in Branksome Grande, enjoying her delicious pasta and salad. These memories will always be vividly etched in me.

Laure, I miss and love you. I can't wait to see you again soon!

Mark Hsu

Hi Laure,

I remember and miss so many things about you.

I remember sitting with you in the living room of my old home in Saratoga after your mom passed away and talking with you about how you were feeling.

I remember all those letters we wrote to each other, claiming CA or NY to be the superior state, and really just taking the chance to make fun of each other.

I remember when we spent time together while you were at Stanford（and while I was at UC Santa Cruz, having been kicked out of UCLA;-）. Our trips to San Francisco to see a comedy show and grab a bite to eat.

I remember the time you helped me buy that outrageous overcoat that I just had to have for me to attain a deep inner sense of peace...or was it just feeding my stupid ego. I'm pretty sure it was the latter...

I remember when I returned the money to you, you laughed and threw it over your head so that the bills cascaded down like little bits of green confetti...

I remember helping you and your dad move into the home in

Saratoga and trying between the three of us to roll out the carpet correctly. Your dad, when realizing we had rolled it out the wrong direction, simply said "Shit," which I thought was one of the funniest things I had ever heard;-）

I remember when you and Kabir took Gabriela and me to that beautiful lunch on that beautiful day at Copacabana at Repulse Bay 6 years ago and how Gabriela and I looked at each other and asked, "Why are we not living in HK with Laure and Kabir and enjoying this kind of life together?" That was the moment we decided that we would move to HK.

I remember the Cajun dinner we had with Nancy and Louis Bowen, Nisa Leung and James Lin at Magnolia to which Nancy brought party favors and Mardi Gras party favors.

I remember you. I remember so many things about you from before all this. I think precisely because of that, I've had such a difficult time adjusting as I always remember these wonderful things and I want to share them with you. I know 100% that you have all these memories but it's so hard for me to see you and not let my sadness and feeling of helplessness overcome me. I guess it's also because I can sense from you how awkward and frustrating communicating with others through the rudimentary spelling system is, which makes me reluctant to try it but, then again, the alternative is to simply not communicate and of course that's much worse.

I will be back in CA mid-Dec and I will definitely come to see you.

I've also asked my mom to find as many photos of us together as possible and will send them to you.

With big hugs from China!!!

Love,

Mark

Melissa Ma

I first met Laure in 1992 walking into my first day at Goldman Sachs, fresh out of college and just like the rest of our analyst class, excited to be starting the real world, but also intimidating by the scale and magnitude of Wall Street and smart, confident people around us. Little did I know then that our meeting that day would later have such a profound effect on my life.

Our Goldman analyst class of 1992 has gone on to have several very high profile success stories, but it was clear to all from day one that Laure was and would ultimately be one of the memorable stars. Not only was she incredibly bright and outgoing, but also approachable and everyone's friend.

After Goldman, we both went to Harvard Business School but were one year apart. While it was great to have her nearby, we were on very different schedules — not only because she was a first year and I was a second year, but more so, because she knew how to have a seriously fun time (while still nailing her classes) and I sadly had to spend more time in the library studying to get passable, but less successful classroom results!

I would say our friendship really took the next level of "closeness" after HBS when she went back to Hong Kong. We lived in the same

apartment building only a few floors apart. We were in our mid 20s, young and single in Hong Kong right around the 1997 handover and had some of the best times I will always remember. There were five "amigos" – Laure, Myself, Tina Lee, May Sung and Debbie Hsu – who were largely inseparable during this time – lots of parties, exotic trips around Asia, hikes, Sunday brunches, poker/card games and late night gab sessions. A truly ideal way to spend one's 20s.

While for totally separate reasons and different career paths, Laure and I ironically also left Hong Kong around the same time in 2000 and landed in San Francisco. While we did not live in the same apartment building this time, we did only live a few blocks away from each other (and now Laure was joined by our old friend from Goldman, Erin Keown, as a roommate). Now it was just too much of a coincidence... fate was clearly leading me to follow Laure.

What I will remember most about this period is (1) celebrating our 30th birthday together on an African Safari — Laure, myself, Erin and Jean Lin and (2) Kabir. While Laure met Kabir at Goldman Sachs in San Francisco, I had known Kabir far longer — I met him first week of freshman orientation in 1988 at Harvard, shortly after he had arrived from India. He went on to be roommates with one of my best friends from Harvard, so we did see each other over the full four years. When she first told me they were dating, I admit I was shocked — I could not have thought of two people more "chalk and cheese". Now, having been with them since the inception of their relationship, I truly can say I understand the phrase "Opposites attract" and how love can conquer all. Over the years, I have watched each complement each other and slowly take on what they value most in each other (and perhaps lack most in themselves). Their commitment to each other to this day is worthy of our utmost respect. I happily admit to Laure today that I was originally "wrong" about Kabir!

In 2002-2003, about 10 years after I had met Laure and our lives had moved in lock step since then, the unthinkable happened. She went back to Hong Kong with Kabir to join her father at Pacific Venture Partners (PVP) and I remained in San Francisco with a new job at Hellman & Friedman. I knew Laure and I would be friends forever, but physical distance, time zones, marriage and the inevitable next phase of life would come between the closeness we had enjoyed for so many many years. It made me very sad at the time.

However, again, fate intervened. Throughout the years, I had been toying with the idea of creating an Asia private equity business but from an LP (Investor) angle, instead of a GP (manager) angle. I had been brainstorming with Rebecca Xu (HBS '97 classmates with Laure and who was also thinking along the same lines) on and off again for years. Market developments and developments in my own career brought this more to the forefront in 2005, when Rebecca and I began to speak and plan in more earnest. By this time, Laure was firmly entrenched in Asia private equity again and was an invaluable resource. For a long time, she was incredibly generous with her time and knowledge to help me and Rebecca formulate our ideas and map out the marketplace. Finally when it came time to pull the trigger, I called Laure for her suggestions on people to join us, thinking she would have great recommendations given her extensive network of relationships. I never dreamed she would have ever been interested in our idea given the successful career path she had been on and seemed to continue to be heading on as a GP. You could have bowled me over with a feather when she said "what about me?"

Long story short, that is how Laure, Rebecca and I started Asia Alternatives. From the get go, we had three huge obstacles in front of us — (1) it was 100% women founded; (2) most investors believed that money could not be made by foreigners in Asia; and (3) this had never been done - create a scalable Asia-dedicated fund of funds in private equity.

It has at no point in our history been an easy ride, but hard work, friendship and a 100% trust-based partnership (with no individual egos), allowed us to persevere. I am proud to say that Asia Alternatives will celebrate its 10th anniversary next year. We manage over $5 billion today, have the distinction of being the largest Asia FoF and have retained all of our original team. Key to our success has been to continue that culture of partnership, trust and putting the firm first – that Laure, Rebecca and I clung to in those tough, early start-up days.

When Laure had her stroke over three years ago, it happened in our office. It was our team that got her to the hospital, stayed by her and the family's side in those first dark days, arranged for her to be transferred to Stanford and also stayed some extended weekends with her at RIC so Kabir could take some time to be back in California with the kids. People then and now still praise us for what we did, saying it was beyond what an employer would be expected to do – I stop them immediately. We are family and you never need to thank or praise family – it was unthinkable for us to have acted any other way.

Today, we are grateful that Laure is still very much a part of the Asia Alternatives' family – she never wanted to give up her role and involvement with us and for that we all benefit. She comes into our San Francisco office for meetings with managers, board meetings, Monday Morning meetings, Investment Committee meetings, etc. and insists on being on the phone when she cannot be in person. She reads and digests all the materials and continues to ask the same, sharp probing questions as she always has, while gracing us with her balanced and sound judgment.

Personally, I have always had a ton of respect and love for Laure, but never more than I do now. Watching her overcome incredible odds to take care of her family, take care of herself and take care of her friends and Asia Alternatives is nothing but breathtakingly inspiring. Laure is my hero.

From that first analyst meeting in 1992 at Goldman, over the last 20+ years, Laure and I have been led on a path together — whether by fate or a higher order, I will never know. What I do know is that our friendship, mutual respect and love for each other and our families will now bind that path forever.

Patrick Hu

We met in ninth grade in French class in Taipei American School（TAS）in Taipei, Taiwan. She was only there for that year but made friends easily. Even then she had a special knack for making people come together in the best possible way. Her best friends at TAS were Shirley Ko and Frances Chan. My good friends, Ulysses Chuang and John Wang, and I used to hang out with the three of them quite a bit. The six of us got along  very well. The year went by quickly. Ninth grade was perhaps a pivotal year for all of us. Adolescence can have that effect. We spent ninth grade summer discussing life and the meaning of life and love, hanging out, listening to Shirley and Laure play Mozart on the piano, watching movies together like Amadeus, and listening to groups like Alphaville,

Reflections on A Changed Life

Chicago, Erasure, and Depeche Mode. I still remember walking the streets of Taipei, with a boombox cradled in my hand (a habit I picked up from my friend Eric Davis), blaring out sappy Chicago songs. Chinese American teenagers roaming the streets of Taipei with romantic American songs blaring usually did cause somewhat of a stir, sometimes perhaps negative. Magical though would be my description of it. We had such joie de vivre. Summer was surely too short. Somewhere in the middle of it, Laure left permanently back to Pleasantville, NY, and Ulysses left at summers end to start boarding school at Exeter.

Unlike these days where Facebook, email, Skype and even out-of-country phone calls are common place, Laure and I managed to kept in touch periodically by surface mail, and in junior year she wrote me a letter from Pleasantville stating her mother had passed away from cancer. I told John, who told Shirley, who told Frances. We were devastated. How could this happen to a beautiful intelligent 40-some year old lady who was the mother of our friend? We each called Laure from Taipei to see how she was. However, our group of friends, no matter how strong our bond, could not help Laure or her sister as much as their friends in Pleasantville. This trial was one that she went through without us. Despite how difficult this was for her emotionally, Laure still put her best foot forward, and marched forward with her life. By the end of senior year, she had offers from top schools in the country and chose Stanford over Harvard for undergraduate. Our paths crossed fleetingly again as I went to Cal Berkeley slightly up the road from her.

Reflections on A Changed Life

Laure is one of those over-achievers that is the envy of everyone. Somehow she is able to do everything, and do it well. At Stanford, this was no exception. She was able to excel in her studies, join a sorority, and clinch a top notch job with the top investment banking firm at the end of college, Goldman Sachs.

Laure is one of those special people that despite her busy schedule, doesn't forget her old friends. I especially remember the call I received from her on Christmas Eve, the first year after college graduation. She was still hard at work at Goldman, and Christmas this first post-college year for most of the intern crowd would be spent at work. It was a lonely, but apparently necessary initiation for the interns. I was hard at work in North Carolina as a research technician as well. It was good to hear her voice – it felt a little bit like we were once again in Taiwan, the good old days, despite the snow in North Carolina or the empty offices in Goldman in New York City.

Life goes by quickly when you work. Looking back, ten years went by in the blink of an eye. In that time, I had finished graduate school as well as medical school. Laure in the meantime had risen through the ranks of Goldman, and gone to business school at Harvard and somehow managed to learn ultra diamond star French culinary cooking in France with the true masters – all in French!

After a few false starts, she eventually met the love of her life, Kabir, who I met later, and I must say, matches her wit for wit, hair for hair in terms of being an overachiever who does things effortlessly well.

They complement each other well, both attractive and charismatic, with IQs and EQs to boot. Furthermore, he went to Harvard undergraduate and then Stanford business school. They were married in Kauai, and although I couldn't go, I was told by Frances and John that it was a beautiful wedding. In typical Laure style, she also had weddings with Kabir in India and Taipei (where her father had relocated back).

Laure started up her own investment company with her two former Harvard business school classmates in Hong Kong. Yet on her highly successful trip to the United States in 2006 to speak to various groups to raise initial funds, she managed to visit some of her old friends such as myself in San Francisco, and John Wang in New York. I think the term third culture kid does apply to all of us, because even though we saw each other rarely throughout this 20-plus-year time period, our bond since those adolescent years in 1984-85 stayed strong. There is a saying amongst the expatriate children who grew up in these English-speaking international high schools that to paraphrase: "In Taiwan we are not viewed as Taiwanese, and in America we are not viewed as Americans." Thus our cultural identity is within our own group of international kids, whatever race that may be. Laure however, takes it to another level, and no matter how far apart we all have been, managed to keep in touch with all of us periodically. She is that type of person, that understands the value of friendship, cherishes it, and maintains it, despite the distance.

Before her stroke, I last had lunch with Laure in Hong Kong in

2007. Her son Ton Ton was perhaps three years old back then, and his vocabulary was spectacular. She knew the importance of good parenting and worked hard at it with him.

When the stroke happened in Hong Kong, I was shocked. Was this a joke? How could it happen to the sweetest of people? My friend, who had suffered so much with her mom passing so early, who had risen to the responsibility of trying to be more than an older sister to her sister, younger by four years, and who was always trying to look out for people other than herself? Finally with her career on the rise, as one of the meteoric rising stars of Asia in the finance world and this is what happens?

Her friends and family gathered to her, testament to the number of good friends she had. Shirley Ko flew from Taiwan to Hong Kong twice to be by Laure's side. She read the Bible to her. Laure's aunt organized a special meditation session of a few hundred monks to pray and chant for her. Her sister, Joan, was constantly by her side, protective, and tried to interpret Laure's body language and facial signs in special sister-to-sister empathy to try to help tell others when she thought her sister was suffering. When she was flown to Stanford one month later, her many friends in California and around the world also came by, including myself.

For all the hard work Laure put into developing her finance background, I too had put into the medical world. I have a PhD in cancer biology and MD from Duke University. I was finishing up the final part of my training as an Interventional Cardiology fellow at UC San Diego in 2010 when the stroke occurred. I place stents in the carotid, vertebral and subclavian arteries, if needed, as well as other arteries in the heart, kidney, and legs. Therefore, I spoke to the Stanford Neurology team in detail as well when I arrived, as per the request of Laure's father, Paul, and her husband, Kabir. However, the brain is the most fragile part of our bodies, more fragile than the heart, and without oxygen for even 3 minutes, the damage can be irreversible. Flow had returned to her brain soon after the stroke, despite the pseudoaneurysm and thrombus, but the damage had already been done. Therefore, frustratingly, it would be pointless to stent at this time.

Laure was a fighter, and somehow survived. After several months of physical therapy, she eventually settled down with her husband and two children in Atherton. Frances Chan (also from ninth grade) flew in from London to see her best friend from old. She too asked a special priest who she knew very well, "His Holiness Grandmaster Lin Yun" from the Black Sect Tantric Buddhism (on par some would say with the Dalai Lama in some respects) to meditate for Laure as well. He did so. Sick himself with a terminal illness, he passed away a few months later at the age of 80.

Laure has confided in me that she has days when she has such a hard time. And I know it is hard for her. She is so gifted in so many ways. She spoke five languages fluently including English, French, Japanese, Chinese and Latin. She plays piano, clarinet and violin to name a few.

Reflections on A Changed Life

To be able to still possess those skills but not to be able to use them must surely be frustrating. Yet… she is alive, and she is able to write this book. Not only through sheer willpower, which she does not lack, but also because she is that special Laure that we so love and adore.

She has changed in some ways. I have told her that she has a new role now, perhaps that of a good listener. To talk to someone with basilar infarct like Laure can be difficult, because if anyone can now stare you down, it would be her. She looks at you patiently while she digests what you are saying. My conversations in the past were probably 70-30. That is she would speak 70% of the time, and I would speak 30% of the time, typical guy style. Since the stroke however, it is now split more like 5-95 with me providing about 95% of the conversation, which makes it harder for me (and possibly many guys) since I like my woman friends to do more of the talking and I chime in as I please with a witty remark here and there. For example, Laure would use her blink language to spell S-H-I-R-L-E-Y and I would tell her everything I knew about my trip back to Taipei and provide some updates about Shirley. I find that I end up telling more to Laure than I have probably every told her in my life (at least since ninth grade). We shared a laugh when I shared this insight. I think people talk to her more, not less. With the silence, often there is a unconscious need to fill the void, that uncomfortable pause, causing one to share more information than perhaps would come out in normal conversation. For better or worse, I think it is true that her numerous friends who have visited her tell her more things than ever.

She has become a confidant and even soothsayer in some ways and communicates critical messages in terse but succinct language as only Laure can.

She tries so hard. Her days are filled with therapy including acupuncture, physical therapy, and speech therapy, and she has visitors constantly. Each time I visit, Kabir has to block some time out so other visitors don't coincide.

Her brain is so active. At her 20 year Stanford reunion 2012, there were several talks about the brain, and stroke research. Laure asked a lot of questions, and had several insightful comments about stem cells and certain signaling pathways. I invited my friend, Stanford researcher Dr. Kang Shen to visit her and discuss various neuronal pathways as well.

Once when I was visiting her, someone asked Laure a question about who is managing the household more, Kabir or her, and she answered that she is managing about 70%. That may seem astounding to others, but to all of us, it is typical Laure. She is definitely her normal self.

As friends, I try to be as much of a friend to her as she has been to me, but she has set the bar high. Even though this period of my own life is extremely busy as I struggle to make my own career blossom, this is a very special friend that I deeply cherish. Even at her busiest, Laure always made time for me. When Laure's helper introduced me again to Ton Ton as a doctor, he point blank asked me if I could make his mother better again. That brought Laure to tears and she made that low pitched wail she makes when she is sad, and I admit I had some water in my eyes as well. And to watch her struggle is hard, but when I see her strapped up with the belt supporting her doing her physical therapy, I know that if anybody can get better, it will be Laure, in typical Laure fashion through hardwork and willpower.

Even if she stays the same, with limited phyical function, I am so glad that she has made her bucket list, because I too need to make a bucket list. Who knows when each of our time on Earth is up? So often we put our own needs aside, and live to help others. Laure, even though she has limited function, is still trying to manage her household, her children, help her sister, help all her friends and once again forget about her own personal happiness in perhaps typical Chinese fashion.

And she is so alive. Her frontal lobes are intact. She processes data as before. Her writing in this book shows such clarity and insight. As Kabir so keenly pointed out, "I just talk to her as I did before the stroke." Laure is still our Laure.

Rev. Joanie Tankersley

My life has been forever changed because of knowing Laure Wang. I have been a Presbyterian pastor for several years, having the opportunity to get to know many people in many different situations. I have never had the privilege of getting to know someone who has been in the kind of radically life-altering condition Laure has experienced.

Friends of hers, who also attend Menlo Park Presbyterian Church, first called me to visit Laure. Upon meeting Laure in the hospital a few weeks after her stroke, I was initially at a loss as to how to be helpful other than to pray for her. I quickly concluded that I needed to far better understand who Laure was regardless of her condition.

What I discovered was an incredibly smart, strong, capable, loving woman whose life was rooted in a solid Christian faith in God. Over the past 4 years I have watched Laure wrestle with her faith wondering why this terrible stroke had happen to her; and yet through it all, I have witnessed her indomitable spirit as she has held onto God's presence in her life. I believe her faith in God has been a major force for good in her life and in the life of her family.

Laure's perseverance, courage and determination to trust God to bring healing to her body, as well as to her soul and spirit, is one of the most remarkable evidences of a person living out her faith in the most

challenging circumstances. I am most grateful for the honor of being a part of Laure's wide circle of friends and admirers as I continue to pray fervently for her complete healing.

　　With deep respect and affection,

Rev. Joanie Tankersley

Sharon Kim

I remember when I was pregnant and after having Gabrielle, meeting some people in my building who would act as if they knew me and would recall to me shared experiences. I brushed off these apparent memory lapses until I met Laure and I realized that there some people in our building had been confusing us. When I met her Laure, I liked her instantly. I think the fact that she was wearing a pair of shoes that I also owned sealed it for me. Before the fashionistas get too excited, they were a boring pair of Franco Sartos, but they were so comfortable.

To me, Laure is always be the mom "in the know". However, she uses her "uber mommy" powers for good and shares her research. She organized a weekly playgroup for our oldest kids. She organized baby swim lessons in our building. She brought me to new play gym openings. She told me about which classes to get my kids wait listed on at pretty much every stage from 0 to 5 years. Even, more recently, when I went to see her in Atherton, she was telling me about the Hopkins summer program.

We still cook a pasta dish with chicken in wine sauce that we learned from Laure. I don't know whether she picked this up whilst being a trainee in the michelin star restaurant in Paris, but I like to think

Laure is swimming with my 3 year old daughter at her 3rd bday party because I was 8 months pregnant with my son Gavin.

that I am eating a Michelin star meal every time we have this for dinner. Seriously, Laure actually did work as an apprentice in a Michelin star restaurant in Paris. I remember that she told me she was eating lunch with a friend and got talking to the chef, and she was asking about Cordon Bleu or other cookery courses, and he offered her to return, and to work in his kitchen. Laure stayed with a friend's mother in Paris, who sounded like an amazing and colorful lady. With a house full of guests, Laure told me of an incident where she woke up in her room with a house guest standing at her door asking (imagine Laure doing a bad American's imitation of a French accent) "I zleep heyuh?" and how he walked away by her valley girl crescendo "NooOOO" unfazed and unembarrassed.

She had made a shaker for Ton Ton with a chopstick, tape, rice, and a yakult container. I never knew where Laure would get the time and energy to do so much. I remember her sharing her annual review templates with me for her nannies. Me and my measly label machine never came close to the organizational pinnacle that Laure is.

Most of my memories of Laure in Hong Kong area around eating and discussing my work-angst merry-go-round internal debate. I remember eating lunch with her at Sevva, perched on top of the Alexandra House. I remember Inagiku at the IFC. She always discovered first my new favorite restaurants in Hong Kong for me. I remember at each of these restaurants discussing my working mom guilt. Both times I visited Atherton, Laure asked me whether I still had "working mom angst". I still do.

She took me to a concert in Hong Kong after I had my second baby and was having a hard time coping. I can't remember the performer or even the genre, but I remember during intermission talking to Laure and feeling content knowing that I had her "in my corner". I am privileged that Laure, "the rock", let herself be vulnerable to me and share with me the sides to us that we obscure from the family Christmas card photo. Its in the fragile state of when we feel the weight of our inadequacy, that bonded us.

I remember feeling nervous the first time seeing her in Atherton. The last time I had seen her was at her baby shower at The China Club before Calliou was born. I was unable to see her before moving to Singapore within months of the stroke. I had thought of her often, but did not have the chance to visit her before 2012. I did not know what to expect. I was amazed to find the same fast-talking Laure with more determination to welcome me and to find out what was happening with me by using the laser attached to her forehead to point to letters taped to a wall so she could spell out words until I could guess her questions. I told her about being sick and all the emotional phases I had gone through, and she wept with me. I returned at Christmas 2013, and she asked whether I was ok referring to our 2012 conversation and she was relieved for me that I was healthy. I told her about missing my flight because my boys' US passports expired and I did not realize that they could not enter with their British passports without a US visa and she shook with side-splitting laughter, knowing it was a organizationally challenged mess I am in the home.

Steve Rehmus

Laure,

Thank you for the privilege to be your friend and to contribute words to your book. You are a remarkable Being. I have genuine affection, trust and respect for you at numerous levels.

Your character strengths have shown through clearly and repeatedly over the years that I have had a connection with you. This opportunity seems a good one to share publicly some of those strengths that have most moved me.

From the earliest days that I have known you, you have been extraordinarily kind to people. Your natural caring instincts have made shown through from the beginning. Even as you've grown more dependent on the care of others, your desire to care for them reciprocally has been there. Thank you for your care for me.

I also greatly appreciate your vitality and zest. Half-hearted is not in your worldview. Your early career energy, your entrepreneurial energy and your healing energy have all been a sight to behold. Many others might feel that a physical limitation like yours would be a legitimate excuse to feel less alive. You have been a model for the opposite. Thank you for being a model for all of us as to what a gift life is, in whatever form it takes.

Reflections on A Changed Life

Thank goodness that your laugh still shines through. Your playfulness and your ability to see the light side of things come through almost whenever I visit. Whenever I've asked you about your state of mind in recent years, I've been impressed at how positive it continues to be. Thank you for being that beacon.

Your courage, while even more apparent since the stroke, has been most striking. Your mom's passing, your early career challenges, your entrepreneurial obstacles, and your post-stroke marathon—all have been a testament to your ability transcend fear. This courage, married with your hope & optimism, is such a remarkable inspiration. My gratitude to you is very real.

Lastly, your sense of a larger purpose to your life and of faith in what we cannot know is a great gift to those of us with less clarity. Since the stroke, I have felt strongly that you have had a striking opportunity to be a model for those of us with fewer challenges. Thank you for giving us a sense of the possible, of meaning even in the midst of substantial obstacles.

You have a very large group of supporters who deeply care about you. I count myself lucky to be among them.

I look forward to a long life of deepening our friendship.

Warmly,

Steve

Reflections on A Changed Life

Suzanne Chu

My husband, Tuan Lam, and Laure first met at Stanford University in 1990 where Laure was the cool Asian with a BMW, and my husband was the geeky guy with a bicycle. They didn't have that much in common back then so their friendship was just cordial.

Things turned around at Goldman Sachs when they were both working in New York as investment banking analysts. Late one midnight, Laure, who was always upbeat, was very stressed because she had a spreadsheet due, and she didn't know how to structure some parts. My husband happened to be in the office and helped her out. That was the start of their real friendship, and the topic of many future conversations. Later, at Harvard Business School where I met my husband, I hadn't met Laure yet, but our network of mutual friends became invaluable.

In 2001, after I married Tuan, and Laure married Kabir, we were all living in Hong Kong. Tuan and Laure had both switched from investment banking to private equity, and they still had much to talk about. Throw in a wine fetish, and we had the start of a Dinner Club that comprised of many friends from Goldman. Those were seriously fun times. In Hong Kong, everyone was lucky to have a helper（ie, a full-time nanny）so we could drink as much as we wanted and stay out as late as we wanted. I didn't speak Mandarin or work in finance, but I still had fun as Laure

always knew how to be friends with everyone and make sure everyone was having a good time, including me.

Little did I know how much Laure would mean to me in 2006 when we gave birth a few weeks apart to our sons, Ryan and Ton Ton, who have done almost everything together from play groups in Hong Kong to their first boarding camp in the Santa Cruz mountains to getting baptized to visiting the White House. Regardless of their proximity to each other (Ryan still lives in Hong Kong and Ton Ton subsequently moved to California), the kids are best friends. Their relationship is so special that it has bonded Laure and I in a special way as well. We are

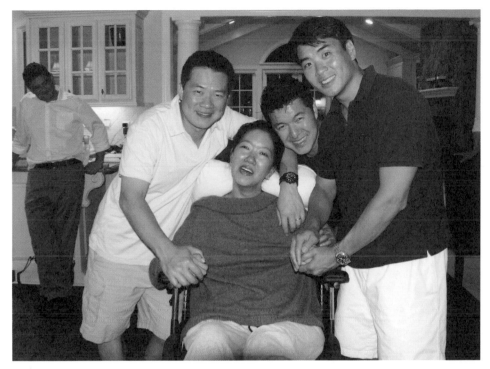

friends for life and it's truly a blessing when you know you have friends that you love and trust. As things continued to look up we both bought homes in Atherton, California, and it seemed that life could not have been better.

Just when you think you are in control, however, God shows you otherwise. I remember getting the call from Kabir one late morning in 2010 saying that Laure was in a coma and that it was serious and that she might die. I couldn't stop crying. How can something like this happen to someone who is so young and so full of vitality? How was her newborn Caillou ever going to get to know his amazing mother?

After calling Tuan and Dinner Club friends there was nothing left to do but pray. So I called my trusted friend Nancy and that's what we did.

The first days at the Queen Mary Hospital in Hong Kong were emotional but hopeful as friends and relatives from all over the world came to visit and pray that Laure would awaken and be fine. On the fourth evening, my prayer warrior friends and I noticed that Laure was trying to open her eyes. It was such a joyful moment and we ran out to tell her dad. While she did open her eyes that night, she didn't speak or move and that was terrifying for her and so heartbreaking to those close to her, especially Kabir and her Dad.

I saw Laure every day in the hospital for about a month until she was well enough to transfer to a stroke specialty center in Chicago. Throughout that month in Hong Kong and the raging fevers that came and went, there was a lot for everyone to reflect on. Was the leak in her brain stem the cause of a neck massage in Shanghai gone wrong? If the hospital had agreed to let Kabir do an MRI, could all of this have been prevented? Does anyone know anyone of influence so that Laure could get the best care? Should long-term care be in the US, Taiwan, Hong Kong or China? How long would it take for Laure to be her old self again??? At least the kids were well taken care of by their loyal nannies, Mely and Dibya, and I was happy to keep Ton Ton occupied.

While in Hong Kong, friends and relatives continued to visit Laure. But as the days passed, it was clear that Laure would need more than physical strength to carry her. She would need an angel and that person was her Aunt Sylvia. Aunt Sylvia, her Dad's sister, cared for Laure everyday in a way that only a mother could. She provided unconditional love, kindness, prayers and the assurance that God was there. We don't always know what His plan is nor do we know the timing of His plan, but we do know that He loves us and heals us.

Even though I walk through the darkest valley, I will fear no evil, for you are with me; your rod and your staff, they comfort me. Psalm 23:4

Psalm 23:4 became almost a mantra for us as we tried our best to help Laure be strong. But after so long in a locked-in state, one's faith can really be tested. Thankfully, Laure chose to be strong in her faith and not feel forsaken despite not having a full recovery. I remember the moment when Laure was finally able to fly to the US. As she was boarding the ambulance in her stretcher to leave the hospital and Hong Kong for the last time, I thought how sad it was to say good-bye to friends, but also how victorious it was for her to be able to leave and work towards recovery at the best stroke center in the US.

It would take many, many hours of hard work and grit to make improvements. In addition, the raging fevers still scared everyone. But, Laure being Laure, has persevered and has been able to host BBQs, take the kids out and enjoy many wine dinners at five-star restaurants.

Since her stroke, my family and I have come to Atherton every Christmas and summer and we have continued to enjoy our times together. There are so many memorable moments, but dinner conversations with the guys –- Tuan, Victor, Kabir, Lewis, Rich, Art and Wen – are always the most hilarious.

I cannot know how it feels to be locked-in, but I know it is one of the most frustrating experiences one could have so I will close this chapter with a few thoughts and prayers for Laure:

May you continue to have unabiding strength, courage, patience and faith.

May your life be harmonious and filled with your children's love and laughter.

May you find comfort knowing that Tuan and I will always be there for your kids as Godparents, Guardians, Auntie and Uncle, or just friends.

May we continue to have many, many more dinner table discussions about nothing and everything.

May you be completely healed on Earth not just in Heaven.

Most importantly, may you always be filled with His unconditional love.

Tara MCann

Laure, when you sent me an email asking me to write a few memories of our times together, I thought it would be an easy assignment. After all, we have so many of them. But time and again, I found myself staring at the computer, and eventually walking away from a blank screen. This happened more times than I care to admit. And I'd kick myself each time. What was it that was so hard about this that I was procrastinating needlessly? And then I realized. There was pain involved. Writing about you reminded me of a time when things were simpler, friendships better, and life limitless. Because, you see, you made life that way for me. And for too many years, due to personal circumstances – both yours and mine – I haven't been able to be near you. And I had forgotten some of these lessons that you had taught me. And by writing this, I have to be honest to myself and look at my life in a way that you would have me look.

But now I'm up against a deadline, and maybe you remember from Stanford, that a deadline helped me to get things done. Remember bringing me coffee after coffee as I attempted to write my entire Honors

Reflections on A Changed Life

Thesis in the last two weeks of senior year? I don't know what I would have done without your encouragement and complete faith that I would achieve my goal. And that faith was always your outlook, a quality from a friend that is precious and rare. But let's start at the beginning...

You probably don't remember this, but we had some classes together in Sophomore year. The classes represented Political Science requirements for me and International Relations requirements for you. Several years later, I do still remember that you were in classes before we even knew each other. I had been in awe of answers you gave in classes. Even as a stranger, your brilliance was obvious.

And then Junior year arrived. As my luck (or lack thereof) would have it, I drew a terrible housing number. I can't say that my parents were thrilled to learn that the board expense they paid had me living in a trailer. Manzanita Trailer Park to be exact. I moved in with my draw mate and found I had two additional roommates. One of whom was you. And I quickly realized that my "terrible housing number" was about to give me my best year yet.

We clicked immediately. It wasn't long before we were sitting around our dining room table, debating fighting in the Middle East or other topical events. Sometimes I felt like I learned more from those moments (or hours, as the case may be) than I did in the classroom. Of course, not everything was intellectual. Boys seemed to take up quite a bit of time, too. Crushes of mine that you always supported. Too many nights outside a certain dorm building of John (I'll save myself the embarrassment of naming names 20+ years later). Or wondering if Jason would ever break up with his girlfriend and notice me. You always were there to listen, support, encourage and make me smile.

Of course, it wasn't long before we discovered another similarity. The same birthday! Twins (but one year apart). January 14 was our day! The year that we lived in the trailers, I was turning 21 to your 20. You made sure to send me into my legal age with a party that involved a bottle of champagne, or maybe two? Somewhere along the line, I had the dazzling idea to see if there were any male "McCann's" in the school directory. If so, my plan was to call and ask him out. That way, I would not need to change my name later if I married him. Makes sense, right? I think you tried to talk me out of that, but without success. A few days later, you came with me to meet Mike McCann, a graduate student who looked like ZZ Top. Future husband he was not. But definitely a funny memory involving you.

Junior year had its share of ups and downs. There was a roommate relationship that did not work out (the one with my draw mate). Preparing for the LSAT's was driving me senseless. And beginning to consider law schools added to the heap of stress that was building. But there was always one constant: your support. I could always lean, and no matter how hard I had to, you were able to prop me up stronger. I remember many nights when just plain old tears turned into tears of laughter. It was a talent you possess, Laure. And I appreciated it so much then, as I do now.

Reflections on A Changed Life

Finally, senior year arrived. With both you and Amy overseas during the draw season, it was up to me to pick our number. Well, if it was one thing in which I was consistent, it was that I always drew a bad number. Senior year landed us in Flo Mo. Not the most glamorous of places, but we sure made the best of it. I remember many late nights with us talking to Greg and Ethan about anything and everything. Of course, I think that's when my great cuisine recipe of chips and cheese was invented. (Still eat them, by the way!... and, yes, Cheerios too!). When I was able to buy an Austin-Healy (for a whopping $400, which was just a forewarning that it would rarely work), we were able to spin around a bit more. Remember going to the Stanford Mall and getting my hair highlighted for the first time with your encouragement? That seemed like a life milestone at the time!

Senior year flew. I just couldn't believe when graduation day arrived. I remember looking at you and sadly realizing that the days of having you but a few rooms away would be over. You'd be headed to Goldman, and I was headed to Los Angeles. While we were all excited about what the future had to bring, I certainly knew I longed for what we had in the past. I knew then that my friendship with you was a special one, and one that could not be replicated.

You and I did do a good job keeping in each other's lives. It was you with whom I spent my bachelorette weekend (Napa Valley in a spa... such a great time). It was you who was the cause of my son taking his first plane ride (at just a few months old) so that I could be at your bachelorette weekend. I remember you visiting us in Park City, Utah and going for a hike. The hike was memorable, because Ton Ton saw snow for the first time… and was in wonderment of it all. And of course, there was the sailing adventure we took together when you came to the Caribbean to sail "Dirty Diapers" with my family and me. I remember how scared I was at the time (I was just learning to sail). But you had the calm demeanor of a person who thought that I was sailing like a pro. I know you didn't really think that, but you wanted to support me… like you always did. We sure took the Virgin Islands by storm (a drink at the Bomba Shack, anyone?) and I was sad when the day came that you needed to leave.

It was with honor that I was a bridesmaid in your wedding. I represented the "Stanford years" and could not have been more proud. We certainly were there for each other's life events. But when it came to the every day, it unfortunately happened that days, weeks and – sadly -- eventually months would pass without us talking. I don't know about you, though, but for me, it still felt like we were always with each other in some way.

I moved to the Caribbean full-time and there, my personal situation deteriorated. There was a part of me that kept telling myself to call you. You were the one who I could always speak to about anything. While we didn't always find a solution, you always could help me find a hope that I couldn't see before. But I knew that when I called you, I would have to share a number of things that were hard for me to discuss. And so I held off. It was during this period that I received an email from Betty Hung. And my heart stopped. The news was unbearable. And I couldn't comprehend. Because you, Laure, to me you were invincible. And it seemed so utterly unfair that something so out of your control could change your world.

And then I realized what I had thought: that you were invincible. And I realized that my tense was wrong. You would remain invincible. I knew that if anyone – absolutely anyone – could tackle your situation, it would be you. And so I did what I rarely did. I prayed. That was something else you taught me: your belief in spirituality. Due to my own personal circumstances, I was not able to be with you in person, but you were certainly in my heart and soul.

When I finally was allowed to leave Puerto Rico and return to the states, we Skype'd. I wanted to see you. I wanted you to see me. And I wanted to introduce you to my son (that you only knew as a baby) and my daughter. But when we Skype'd, something interesting happened. We just saw each other and shed tears. There was very little conversation. But it seemed right. Because we never needed conversation to understand each other before. When I hung up, my daughter asked me, "Who was that again?" And I said, "Sadie, that is the most special friend I have ever had… and I can only hope that you will find someone like her in your lifetime."

So, see Laure? I didn't mean to not write this for so long. I just found it to be such an eye-opener of how life should be. Friendships should mean something. There should always be hope in any situation. And life should be limitless. These are all lessons that you taught me while at Stanford. These are all lessons that you are teaching me again. Even from far away, even without telephone calls or regular emails, you are in my heart guiding me. And for that, I am truly blessed.

I love you, Laure.

Vanessa Rocha

I didn't know Laure prior to her injury, but as time passed I felt as if I did. Hearing stories from her sister growing up, her crazy Stanford days, her 21st birthday with Joel, her traveling adventures with friends, meeting Kabir, planning her wedding (which includes the time her dad hugs her), getting pregnant unexpectedly while starting Asia Alt. and then April 26, 2010. I'd heard all the stories from friends and from her, I really felt like I had a clear picture of Laure before April 2010.

Reflections on A Changed Life

I met Laure in May of 2012. I started working for her as a nanny to her two boys. Eventually I became her caregiver, and I had a great connection with Laure. We thought alike in many ways. We shared stories, laughed, played pranks on others and eventually she played pranks on me. People on the outside might look at Laure and feel bad for her and create an image of her life. In reality, I see her just as any other person without a disability. She might not be mobile like I am or communicate what we see as the norm, but she lives life just like us. I am with her for half her day and a big part of my day is usually laughs and stories of her travels which end up in uncontrollable laughter from both of us. As sad as you might think Laure is, I can assure you that she is happier and living life more than some of us who do not have physical limitations. Laure is not only my client or employer, she is now a friend whom I have truly grown to love. Thank you for the stories, laughs, and opportunities you have given me.

Part Five

Laure

241

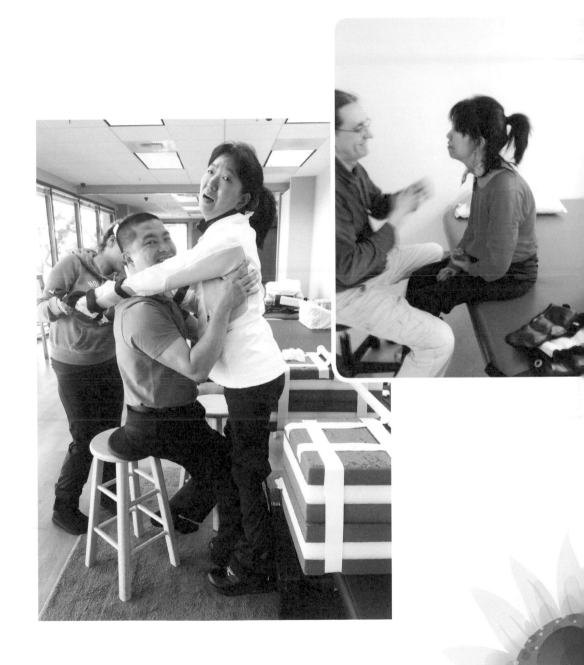

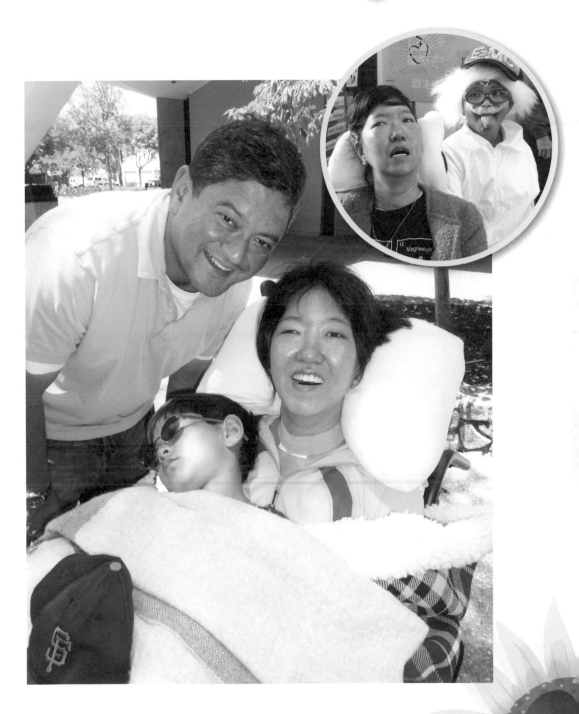

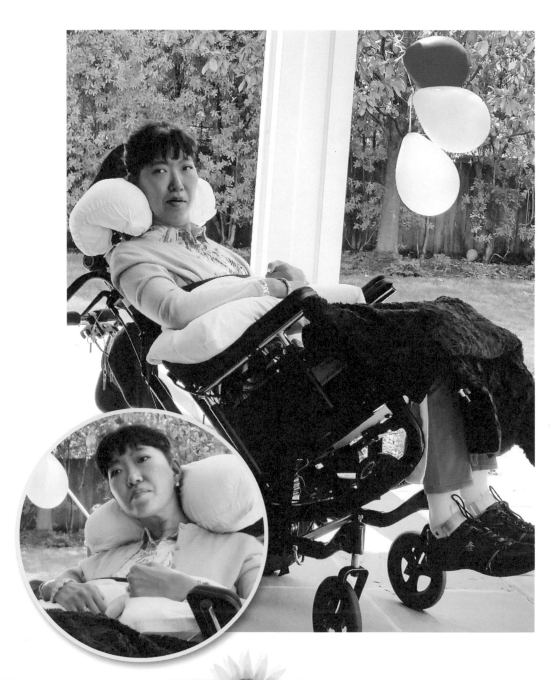

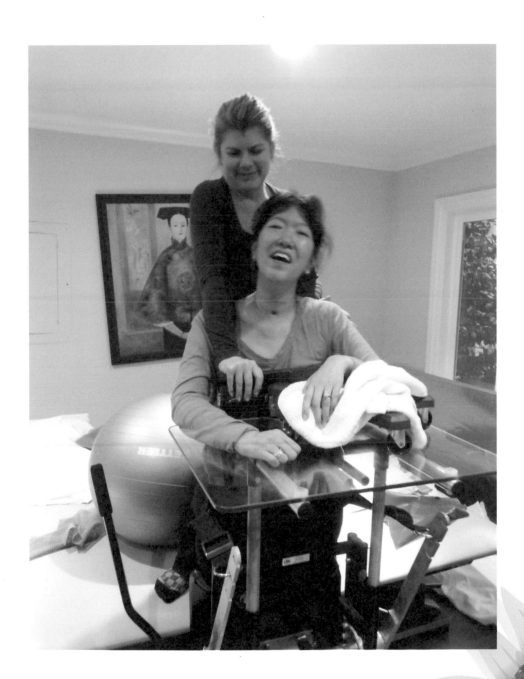

Family

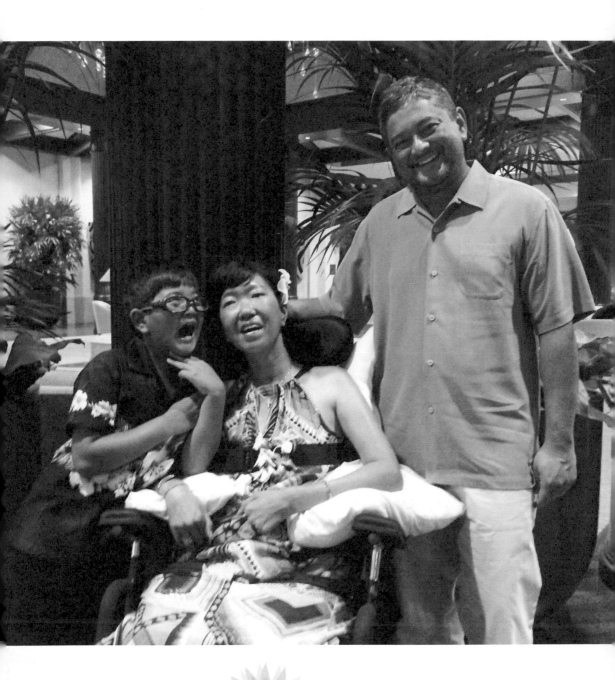

Part Six

王樂怡 躍居亞洲募資女王

創投大老王伯元之女

低迷中尋寶 創投瞄準三高

【記者賴育漣／台北報導】金融風暴狂襲全球，各國市場都傳出募資不易的消息，國內創投耆老王伯元之女王樂怡、亞洲最大的獨立私募綜合投資基金Asia Alternatives，本月初宣布AACP II基金超額募集，原定募集8.5億美元，結果募到9.5億美元。

這次募集的是Asia Alternatives第二檔基金，第一檔AACP 1去年5月完成募集，資金總額為5.15億美元；資金主要來自全球的機構法人與戰略投資人，包括政府及企業的退休基金、慈善資金、保險資金等。

第二檔基金超額募集，資產規模比第一檔多了84%，且絕大多數的資金來自第一檔基金的投資人，顯示Asia Alternatives經營績效受病投資人肯定。王樂怡身為Asia Alternatives創辦人兼董事總經理，她說，感謝原始投資人再度支持。

Asia Alternatives總部設在香港，國年由王樂怡與兩位也讀哈佛大學的同學馬琪薇、徐紅江共同創辦，以投資亞洲私募基金為優先方向，現已有19名員工，以Fund of fund的模式，在亞洲區興出色的基金合作，建立多元化的投資組合，投資觸角遍及亞洲12個國家。

熟悉王的私及王樂怡的創投業界人士指出，王樂怡表現非出於藍，之前有到父親身處創投募資相當辛苦，創業後因而選擇慎募資門鑑較低，現已有19名員工，晉身為創投的新金主，訊記Asia Alternatives之前，她就已有投資銀行豐富及Warburg Pincus的專業歷練，非常熟悉亞洲創投產業的脈動。

Asia Alternatives超額募資，創投高層認為，顯示雖然全球資金逐動緩慢，但只要專業度及績效表現亮麗，投資人還是願意加碼。

【記者賴育漣、呂淑美／台北報導】台股5520之後重挫，市場趨閑，創投近期趨低入市操便宜。怡和創投總裁理楊邦彥表示，創投基金資上市櫃股票原有汰淘選制，現在則沒有限制，加上投資未上市櫃股票已不能享有投資抵減，創投買賣上市櫃股票已成為常態。

楊邦彥說，目前市場上香遍認為價已超跌，本益比最低跌至九至十倍，股價跌破淨值的公司很多，這時創投進場買進上市櫃公司的股票，並沒有內潛的不保正案，或者是擾亂市場等問題。

他說，創投對產業和部分公司更了解珍惜他投資機構，倒投投資上市櫃股票，更考慮是否會有內線交易的問題。

【記者呂淑美、賴育漣／台北報導】經濟不景氣，創投現階段到底都投資哪些產業或公司？一位創投操盤手表示，現階段以投資「價值型投資標的」為主，產業能見度高、現金部位較高、現金流量數高等三高公司，目前創投資兩趨較低。

業者分析，明年有很多公司的可轉換公司債（CB）陸續到期，屆時石還不出錢，將會生流動性風險機，現階段投資宜選擇流動性高的公司。

在產業能見度方面，創投業者表示，傳統產業中以具有大陸、台灣通路概念最多主，例如：就一、大成、麗嬰房、潤泰全等，目前在大陸及台灣都有龐大的通路；現金流入量大且數利穩定；自行車業相關公司，應是未來成長幅度也有二到三成。

但創投業者表示，今年投資應興開屬氣循環股，他認為，平頭包括鋼鐵、水泥等原物料股，現金流入雖較重新正，曲價下跌，顯示市場需求少，經濟景氣不振，預料航運股也不好。

產業能見度高、現金部位高及現金流量高公司。

隨著股價慘澹滑落，創投業者表示，股市大跌，許多人壓力的大，許多疾病都出現了，生技醫療產業前景看好，但仍會以投資國外生技股為主，國內可看墨墨太多。

不景氣下，許多公司會尋求進口設備替代，太陽能設備、光電設備業者，過去都以精質日、德、美等機器設備為主，但如今不景氣，為了削減設備成本，可能回頭向國內好的設備廠採購。

創投者看好，未來企業跨國新流潮，明年破產、整併的公司會愈來愈多，這樣的現象從今年第四季就會出現，很多公司目前無法從銀行借到錢，倒閉的風險非常高。

Asia Alternatives Management LLC
創始人及董事總經理王樂怡，吸金能力超強，近日全球經濟不景氣，投資信心低迷。她推出的新基金卻募爆。
（本報系資料庫）

工商時報　http://news.chinatimes.com　萬花筒　中華民國97年5月8日　星期四　A5

虎父靚女
金融伶俐3千金

2　王樂怡帶資金投資台灣　老爸驕傲

陳碧芬、孫彬訓／台北報導

創投之父王伯元的千金—王樂怡帶著海外資金投資台灣銀行業與高科技業，王樂怡指出，會去有意投資的公司訪談，成為這些公司的策略性投資人，未來希望藉著這個投資平台，提高台灣金融機構的吸引力，及再創造新的高科技龍頭公司。

和哈佛同窗一起創業的王樂怡，二年內經手管理的國際資金達到15億美元，昨天首度在國內公開投資理念，父親怡和創投董事長王伯元就坐在檯下，滿場微笑地專心聆聽。

首度在父親面前演講，王樂怡直說，「

在國外，已有相當多次在父親面前演講的經驗，這次是第一次在台灣，感覺不太一樣」。為了擔心講得不好，從小在美國長大的她，事前暫時使用英文，一次好的中文，日文和法文，都先放到一邊。

王樂怡目前是ASIA ALTERNATIVES MANAGEMENT LLC創始人及董事總經理，以香港為營運據點，此次應允AVCJ為台灣私募股權與創業投資論增站台，是2006年自行創業以來的台灣處女秀，針對台灣科技業的股價表現、創投業的投資績效，侃侃面談，因為這些都是她自幼因父親關係而接觸。唸史丹福大學時身處矽谷環境，更

是加值她的國際架勢。

王伯元說，王樂怡就是看到他做創投太累了，所以想改走私募業，他非常以女兒為傲。王樂怡經歷高盛、Warburg Pincus的專業歷練後，與另外二位哈佛女同學馬現麗、Rebecca Xu一起創業時，即走GP（募集資金）和LP（國際投資）雙軌發展，前者要做到類似私募基金的大型規模，後者接受歐美退休基金委託，需同時展現可信任度與投資專業。

王樂怡昨天談起投資台灣，她認為國內政治氛氛越來越好，外資對台灣很有信心，讓扮演居中角色的她游刃有餘。

王樂怡　58年次

怡和創投集團董事長
王伯元之女

最高學歷：
美國哈佛大學商學院MBA

經歷： 怡和副投美國公司
、高盛、Warburg Pincus

現職： Asia Alternatives
Management LLC 創始人暨
董事總經理

王樂怡鑽進台灣創投

陳碧芬／台北報導

經濟景氣低迷，正是國際投資好手最積極的時候。甫成功募集9.5億美元的國際私募業者王樂怡昨天表示，此波全球金融危機讓歐美投資人終於「看清楚」，包括台灣在內的亞洲地區，才真正值得投資，此區內的創投基金、股權收購、增長和發展型企業和特殊房產，都全面納入未來3年的投資標的。

其中，主力投資在高科技業的台灣創投基金，正面臨產業重整的關卡，國際私募圈，現正熱中組成專門收購台灣創投基金的Secondary Fund。王樂怡表示，創投業明年會發生大洗盤，尤其是在今年底科技業財報結算之後，也是很多創投票到最後決定的時候，可能會是所有資產先殺價50%，再談出售。

王樂怡：歐美金主將加碼在亞洲的投資，台灣創投業明年會發生大洗盤。

據創投公會統計，國內創投業累計資本額約1765億元，已連續5年成長停滯，且創投基金規模偏小，平均每家創投年度投資金額僅7千萬元，但因各業者所投資的科技公司均為台灣最核心的產業價值，如聯發科、友達等，國際私募業正是看上創投業口袋裡的寶藏。

王樂怡為ASIA ALTERNATIVES MANAGEMENT LLC創始人暨董事總經理，這家亞洲最大的獨立私募綜合投資基金，是由她和哈佛同窗馬麗麗和徐紅江於2006年共同創立，3年來2次成功募集5.15億美元、9.5億美元，金主多是公共和企業的退休養老基金、慈善基金會，還包括美國加州理工學院等的大學捐贈基金，且2連續2次都投資AACP，就是肯定這3位國際投資女傑對亞洲市場的熟悉。

王樂怡昨天在接受本報專訪時表示，歐美金主經過此次金融危機的教訓，現在完全認同要調增在亞洲的投資，但不希望都只把錢放在股市，而是要能把資金導入產業或特殊房地產，維持至少3年的投資期。經濟復元之後必定邁利可期，如今拜股價的便宜，投資者可以放情挑選，從中東、印度到日本，遍地黃金。

台灣的部份，王樂怡認為，企業重整、股權收購是國際投資者最有興趣，但絕對沒有以出口為主的科技製造業，主要還是內需導向，且有品牌可以兩岸操作槓桿的產業。至於創投基金的收購，她表示，台灣創投業所投資的科技公司雖然有優勢，但現在已面臨股價重挫，創投產業規模也已受傷，要在此時進行再籌資是不可能，讓國際投資者抓到進入台灣市場的機會。

明年IPO家數將掛零

陳碧芬／台北報導

投資法人、創投業所追求的投資獲利，當然是標的企業的初次掛牌（IPO）。Asia Alternatives董事總經理王樂怡昨天表示，根據目前的全球市況，公司內部已調整手上投資企業的明年IPO數目為「零」，「如果真的有公司順利IPO，那就是我們的BONUS！」

追蹤統計IPO情況的湯森路透（Thomson Reuter）和中國清科公司（Zero2IPO），原先預估IPO可能萎縮4至6成，天天都接觸資本市場的王樂怡，預估情況明顯更為保守。

清科指出，綜合中國與海外市場，今年第3季中國新企業成功IPO的家數減少62%，公開募資則較去年大幅減少95%。湯森路透則統計美

國市場，IPO數目減少39%，兩個機構均認為，明年的情況應持續走低。

王樂怡強調，儘管全球信用緊縮導致IPO不順，但以美國20年來的投資市場，歷經了亞洲金融風暴、網路泡沫等多次景氣循環，愈是可以在景氣谷底有所表現的新企業，愈是具有投資價值，且長期表現傑出，「現在能夠募到資金的人，將掌握最好的投資時機。」

王樂怡認為，現在歐美金主熱中於調增投資亞洲的比例，由於各基金的規模都以億美元起算，就算調增1%在亞洲市場，都是很大筆的金額，未來若這些資金競逐可以成功IPO的新企業，市場將掀起難得的競價效應。

当前位置：首页 > > 投资行业 > VC访谈

Asia Alternatives合伙人王乐怡：FOF投资PE将较保守

发布时间：2008-11-24 10:54:00   来源：ChinaVenture   作者：Vincent

融资情报   融资事件   并购事件   上市事件   基金募资   更多VC访谈

相关行业：投资行业

编者按：Asia Alternatives，亚洲最大的独立私募综合投资基金（private equity fund of funds），近日宣布成功完成Asia Alternatives Capital Partners II, LP基金（"AACP II"或"II期基金"）的募集活动，共筹集到9.5亿美元的资本。ChinaVenture有幸采访到了Asia Alternatives创办人暨董事总经理王乐怡女士，王女士对募资、GP选择、人民币基金等问题发表了一系列精彩的观点。

ChinaVenture：请先简单介绍一下Asia Alternatives Management LLC及此次募集的新基金的情况。

王乐怡：Asia Alternatives是投资亚洲的一个FOF，投资基金包括Venture Capital、Growth Capital、Buyout及distressdebt，也包括房地产基金。我们的投资区域涵盖整个亚洲，包括日本、韩国、中国大陆、台湾、香港、澳大利亚、印度。

我们2006年开始三个人一起创业，我（Laure L.Wang王乐怡）、Rebecca Xu（徐红江）、Melissa J.Ma（马晶丽），我们本来在Goldman Sachs就认识，后来在哈佛商学院也是同学。我们都是不多都有10年的经验在私募投资这个行业里面，就决定要出来创立Asia Alternatives Management LLC。

我们最近close的这个基金是9.5亿美元。我们第一个基金是5.15亿美元，那是2007年的时候final close的。谈到募资，现在的大部分的募资都比较困难，比较幸运的是我们的第一个基金有很强的投资者背景，第二个基金的投资者超过85%都是第一个基金的投资者，需要找的新的投资者并不太多。第二个基金也超过我们8.5亿美元的意门目标。但我们第一个基金其实还是比较难，因为我们那时候是第一次出来，一个新的团队，人家也不知道这个FOF是什么行业，而且我们三个人是没有一起做过事的，所以他们就看得比较严。

ChinaVenture：您第一期基金投资了中国许多TOP基金，像CDH、SAIF、GSR，这些投资履历是不是也对您募集新基金有帮助？

王乐怡：当然会有，我们的目标就是想投亚洲最好的这些基金，我们设一个目标是TOP10，就是全亚洲10%最好的基金。很多人会讲最好的25%，我们的目标就比较高。像中国大陆，我们都是找有最长的历史，最专注的基金，他们往往可以真正达到他们的目标，得到一个很好的回报。我们可以和这些最好的基金合作，我们的投资者看着我们可以步

Charmed by the East

Funds of funds mushroom in Asian private equity

Excitement stirred in the Asian private equity fund management industry when Asia Alternatives Management LLC ('Asia Alternatives') announced the final closing of its maiden Asian fund of funds. Asia Alternatives Capital Partners LP greeted the industry with a final size at US$515 million and took the crown as the largest Asia-focused fund of funds. The announcement came only weeks after Axiom Asia Private Capital achieved its closing at US$440 million. Within this short space of time, an additional US$850 million (fig. 3) has come into the Asian private equity fund of funds industry that is eagerly courting aspiring fund managers. Significantly, Asia Alternatives Capital Partners is an embodiment of a revised approach of institutional investors to Asian private equity, which has now proven that it is a viable investment model.

The Independent

Similar to many other Asian funds that have recently achieved their final closings during the past year, Asia Alternatives Capital Partners is another illustration of institutional investors' insatiable appetite for private equity assets in the region. With an original target size of US$350 million, Asia Alternatives Capital Partners' final closing sum ballooned to US$515

million. It is not only a display of investors' absolute confidence in the newly-established management team, but also an affirmation that institutional investors are adopting a more pragmatic view in making their allocations to funds seeking opportunities in the East.

It has long been the universal requirement from the institutional investor community that founding partners of a first time fund management team must have had working relationships preceding the launch of their own venture. This caveat did not appear to apply to Asia Alternatives. Its founding partners were engaged in different capacities prior to formation of their own firm. Ms Melissa Ma was a director with Hellman & Friedman, an elite buyout firm based in USA, while Ms Rebecca Xu held responsibilities as a senior investment officer at the International Finance Corp.. The third partner, Ms Laure Wang was a general partner of Pacific Venture Partners headquartered in Taiwan (fig. 4). While Ms Ma is a recent entrant to Asian private equity, over the years her two partners have cultivated an extensive network in Asia, especially in the Greater China region. Perhaps one of Asia

Alternatives' most convincing assets is Ms Xu's lengthy association with CDH Investments since the latter's inception years. CDH Investments' legendary success in China's alluring private equity market is an endorsement of Asia Alternatives' ability to identify aspiring fund managers.

In granting Asia Alternatives the mandate as the ideal team to scout for promising fund managers in Asia's complex private equity landscape, institutional investors placed their vote of confidence in the three founding partners. Their diversified background, in-depth knowledge of Asian private equity, and profound understanding of US institutional investors expectations are powerful combination of factors that convinced investors to loosen their purse strings. It comes as no surprise that two of Asia Alternatives Capital Partners' limited partners, California Public Employees' Retirement System and Oak Hill Investment Management, took an unusual move in commenting publicly on their partnership with Asia Alternatives. In an industry that guards investment rationale as a private affair, the highly visible statements coming from these two

Growth of Asian Private Equity Funds of Funds (2004 - May/2007)

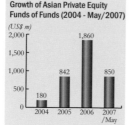

Fig. 3   *Source:* ASIA PRIVATE EQUITY REVIEW

Dossier of Asia Alternatives Founding Partner

Founding Partners:	Ms Melissa J. Ma, former director at Hellman & Friedman LLC
	Ms Laure L. Wang, former general partner of Pacific Venture Partners
	Ms Rebecca Xu, former senior investment officer at the International Finance Corporation
Fund Name:	Asia Alternatives Capital Partners, LP
Target Size:	US$350 m, closes at US$515 m in May 2007
Key Investors:	California Public Employees' Retirement System (CALPERS)
	California Institute of Technology
	Comprehensive Financial Management
	MassMutual Asia
	Oak Hill Investment Management
	Ontario Municipal Employees Retirement System
	Pennsylvania State Employees' Retirement System (SERS)
	F. Warren Hellman, founder of private equity firm Hellman & Friedman LLC
	Arthur Rock, a leading venture capitalist

Asia Alternatives = Asia Alternatives Management LLC

Fig. 4

Source: Asia Alternatives Management LLC
Graphic: ASIA PRIVATE EQUITY REVIEW

*PEI*Asia

The magazine for private equity in Asia, Australasia and the Middle East

www.PEIAsia.net
June 2007, Issue 11
MICA (P) 078/04/2007   ISSN 1751-2948

**JAPAN
SPECIAL**

*A buyout market
picks up speed*

- **Up front**
  Asia Alternatives' impressive debut
- **Blackstone's China deal**
  Big implications for private equity
- **Turnaround investing**
  Getting Asian workouts right

- **Middle East**
  Bahrain on the chase
- **Bain Capital in Asia**
  Armed with a big team and
  $1 billion
- **Venture capital**
  Kleiner Perkins arrives in China

PEI

A PRIVATE EQUITY INTERNATIONAL PUBLICATION

Fund of funds debutantes

*Meet one of Asia's first-ever home-grown funds of funds: Asia Alternatives in Hong Kong. Earlier this year, the firm's long-anticipated maiden fund closed on $515 million. When all the work was done, founders Melissa Ma, Laure Wang and Rebecca Xu made time for a wide-ranging conversation with **Sharon Lim**.*

As debut funds go, Asia Alternatives has had a brilliant start. In May, the firm announced the final close on a $515 million fund of funds, raised from a group of heavyweight institutions that many first-time managers can only dream of attracting.

Headquartered in Hong Kong with additional offices in San Francisco and Beijing, the firm has already made commitments to more than 10 Asian private equity partnerships, including leading names such as CDH China Fund III, SAIF Partners Fund III and MBK Partners in South Korea. Other GPs in the portfolio include Capital Today, Hony Capital, Clearwater Capital, Nexus Capital and NEA Indo-US.

The firm's success is reflective of an important trend: with private equity gaining momentum in Asia, institutional investors who haven't made allocations to the region yet are increasingly relying on local professionals to identify the best opportunities.

From left to right: Rebecca Xu, Melissa Ma, Laure Wang

Until quite recently, investors from North America and Europe looking for Asian private equity exposure would typically knock on the doors of international capital aggregators such as HarbourVest Partners and Pantheon Ventures, two groups that have had offices in Asia for many years. Today, these pioneers have to contend with a lot more competition. Not only have they been joined by international rivals such as Adams Street Partners, AXA Private Equity, Capital Dynamics and Partners Group, all of which opened up offices in Hong Kong or Singapore in the past two years. In addition, a number of local funds of funds have emerged, notably Axiom Asia Private Capital in Singapore, Squadron Capital in Hong Kong – as well as the team at Asia Alternatives.

The level of competition, says a rival fund of funds proprietor, makes it all the more "impressive" that Asia Alternatives has managed to garner so much support

"Our job is to scour all the markets and managers to only look for those opportunities where the LPs are more than getting compensated for the additional risk they are taking by investing in Asia."

from investors. "Just how did they manage to raise all this money?" he asks.

DRAWING ATTENTION

Asia Alternatives may be a new firm in a young market, but insiders have been watching its progress for some time. One obvious reason for the relatively high profile is that founders Melissa Ma, Rebecca Xu and Laure Wang are all

female, which undoubtedly makes them stand out from their peers. Another factor right from the beginning has been the fact that the principals were already well known in Asian private equity circles before they joined forces to set up the firm.

Prior to teaming up with Xu and Wang, Ma was a director at US LBO investor Hellman & Friedman in San Francisco. Before joining H&F, she worked for McKinsey and Goldman Sachs, spending time in New York, San Francisco and Hong Kong.

Xu first met Ma at McKinsey before heading off into the public sector to join the International Finance Corporation, an investment arm of the World Bank based in Washington, DC. As head of the IFC's Asian investment portfolio and a founding member of the group's private equity programme, Xu reviewed more than 225 private equity fund investment opportunities and committed over $150 million of capital to Asian funds.

In February 2004, Ma and Xu bumped into each other at a conference and discovered that they both had an entrepreneurial itch to scratch. Swapping notes about private equity's taking shape in Asia over lunch, they came to the conclusion that an independent local fund of funds would serve the growing needs of an international clientele.

Wang, a former colleague of Ma's at Goldman Sachs, joined the team a year later. At the time, she was a general partner at Pacific Venture Partners, an $800 million pan-Asian venture capital firm with operations in China and the US. Before joining Pacific Venture Partners in 2002, she had been with Goldman for eight years, working in a number of private equity-related roles.

The idea of a fund of funds appealed to Wang immediately, and so she agreed to become the third partner. Her operational experience came in handy to set up the necessary infrastructure.

GETTING STARTED

During those formative conversations at the very beginning, the three founders felt strongly that the time was right to go into business with each other to build an Asian fund investment operation. In their previous roles, all of them had had ample opportunity to watch from close range where the market was heading.

"Stories of successful local GPs really emerged only about three to five years ago, and there were few notable Asian investors at the time. But investments over the early 2000s soon attracted the interest of Western investors, which gave rise to demand for a local insider, someone who is on the ground," says Ma in an interview with *PEI Asia* in early May.

Xu, a Chinese national (Ma and Wang were born in North America, but all three founders are fluent in Mandarin; Wang also has working knowledge of Japanese and French), remembers spending a lot of time with US limited partners asking her questions about Asia. "These investors were so busy in their home markets and lacked the resources to explore opportunities in Asia. [We knew] we had the skill set, knowledge and passion to do it for them," she recalls.

Wang's experience at Pacific Venture Partners had also been very similar: "I was in Shanghai at the time and getting a lot of visits from investors who felt that I had a special insight into local GPs." Wang too was asked a lot of questions about Chinese private equity and China more broadly ('How many provinces are there?' was one she remembers), and it didn't take long for Wang to realise that here was very interesting business opportunity.

In the second half of 2005, the trio put together a business plan and agreed the division of labour: based in San Francisco, Ma would be responsible for fundraising and investor relations; Wang and Xu would co-head the firm's Hong Kong base; all three would sit on the investment committee.

KEEN INVESTORS

Ma's operating out of San Francisco – she spends her time shuttling back and forth between the two regions – has a very practical advantage: proximity to the firm's investors, as well as some important friends.

More than 60 percent of the firm's investors are based in North America. CalPERS, Pennsylvania State, California Institute of Technology and Massachusetts Mutual Life are among the firm's US clients. Canada's OMERS Capital Partners invested also.

Before the institutions piled in, some influential individuals threw their weight behind the project. Ma's former boss Warren Hellman and Arthur Rock, a well known figure in Silicon Valley venture capital with close ties to Hellman's firm, both made equity investments in the firm's management company. Oak Hill Investment Management Asia Investors, a vehicle overseen by former CalPERS private equity chief Rick Hayes, did the same.

In closing Fund I on $515 million, Asia Alternatives not only exceeded the $350 million target, but also smashed through the $450 million hard cap. C.P. Eaton acted as placement agent. The partners are convinced that the decision to raise a slightly larger fund was correct. Says Ma: "The fund size was ultimately based on what we can invest, not how much we can raise."

Was being an all-female cast of decision-makers ever an issue during the fundraising? The women confirm that a number of investors had gender-related reservations, but only a small number of potential LPs turned down the proposition.

Xu: carefully chosen funds

Wang: from GP to LP

strategy to focus primarily on Greater China, India, Japan and South Korea. A bottom-up approach is used to identify the best performers in these markets.

According to Ma, the role of Asia in a private equity portfolio is not just to provide geographic diversification. She says: "We don't have a top-down view that determines that China will be given a specific percentage allocation. Instead, there are quarterly reviews and analyses of each market, to provide flexibility to change the portfolio mix. We also conduct a bottom-up screening of managers. Our job is then to scour all the markets and managers to only look for those opportunities where the LPs are more than getting compensated for the additional risk they are taking by investing in Asia."

Says Ma: "There was a small group of investors who were not familiar with the Asian culture or our network and unfairly determined we could not be successful in what they viewed as a fairly male-dominated industry. If I had met many LPs who turned us away because of our gender at the start of our fundraising, I admit it would have been demoralising. We did encounter some towards the end, when we were cutting back allocations. So while their reaction was a disappointment, it wasn't a big blow."

And Xu: "If we were going to do direct investments in Japan, I could imagine the challenges in trying to break into the market. But when we talk to GPs, they are essentially looking for LPs who understand what they are doing. They tend to be gender-blind."

SEEKING ALPHA

Each partner's experience and personal connections within the region contributed to shaping the fund of fund's

> "There is a lot of deal competition that could put pressure on returns. But we pick GPs that have market downturns on their minds."

As a general rule, 80 percent of Asia Alternative's capital will be invested in growth capital funds in China and India and mid-market buyout funds in Japan and Korea, leaving the remainder for venture capital, distressed debt and other special situation funds, says Xu.

Many of the funds picked so far are China-focused, partly because several Chinese managers that the team knew well were out raising capital at the same time. Fewer commitments have been made to India, as Asia Alternatives continues to track developments in that market. "We don't start looking at a fund only when the PPM comes out. It is an ongoing process as we monitor the deals they have done, even sometimes getting

to know their families along the way," Wang says.

Regardless of where the firm invests, it has a preference for partnerships owned by independent Asian groups that may be raising their third or fourth funds. Ma is conscious that the most successful local teams are now raising follow-on funds that are substantially larger than their predecessors – a phenomenon she says that bears close watch and potential caution: "Many of the firms are still quite young and questions remain if the teams are structurally ready to manage this much money."

Adds Xu: "Some first-time managers may be too eager to invest and could end up investing too quickly." Thus far, the firm has only invested in one partnership with more than $2 billion in commitments.

Xu explains that to warrant attention from the firm, fund managers need to be able to show a track record, consistency in strategy, team stability and growth. They need to show that they appropriately incentivise their investment teams.

Reflections on A Changed Life

> *"Many of the firms are still quite young and questions remain if the teams are structurally ready to manage this much money."*

And they also need to find a way to impress Wang, who crossed over to being a fund investor after thirteen years as a fund manager, a move that puts her "in a better position to evaluate GPs" she feels. It also made the obvious candidate for looking after clients that are interested in co-investment.

The same rules that apply to general partners seeking capital commitments from Asia Alternatives are also applied to the firm itself, Xu adds: "In front of our LPs, we are a GP too. I have seen so many first-time emerging market managers, and now that I am part of a new fund, my appreciation of what one has to do to build a partnership has become much deeper."

LOOKING AHEAD

With the first fund raised and the portfolio having taken shape already, Asia Alternatives is now in a position to think about the opportunities and challenges that lie ahead.

One issue is the sheer speed with which Asian private equity has evolved in recent years. The market is currently populated with a significant number of first-time funds including many being raised by practitioners who haven't been in private equity before. In such an environment, GPs and LPs alike need to be treading carefully.

Asked whether 2006 and 2007 vintage funds could suffer from all the excitement and bullishness around them, Xu replies: "I would be worried if I hadn't chosen my funds carefully. There is a lot of deal competition that could put pressure on returns. But we pick GPs that have market downturns on their minds."

The Asia Alternatives ladies are confident that the managers in their portfolio have the ability to clear the hurdles of the future. In conversation, the three come across as thoughtful and immensely passionate when sharing their views about their business. Says Ma: "I am having a great time. This is truly a dream come true."

Given the success the firm has had so far, it is not surprising that the founders' enthusiasm is so readily forthcoming. ∎

Ma: West coast network

ASIA ALTERNATIVES AT A GLANCE:

Year of inception: 2005
Debut fund: $515 million closed in May 2007
(target $350 million; hard cap $450 million)
Offices: Hong Kong, Beijing, San Francisco

Partners: Melissa Ma, Laure Wang, Rebecca Xu

Founding investors with minority stakes:
F. Warren Hellman; Arthur Rock; Oak Hill Investment Management; Asia Investors

Selected limited partners:
CalPERS
Omers Capital Partners
Pennsylvania State Employees' Retirement System
California Institute of Technology
Comprehensive Financial Management
Massachusetts Mutual Life Insurance Company
MassMutual Asia
MassMutual Japan

Selected general partner groups in the portfolio:
Capital Today
CDH China
Clearwater Capital
MBK Partners
Hony Capital
Nexus Capital
NEA Indo-US
SAIF Partners

ASIA

WONDER WOMEN GET TO WORK AT ASIA ALTERNATIVES

On the fund of funds circuit, word has it that the newly formed Asia Alternatives Management is moving in on a first close by the end of July. The group, founded early this year by a

Laure Wang   *Rebecca Xu*   *Melissa Ma*

female powerhouse team of private equity professionals Melissa Ma, Laure Wang, and Rebecca Xu, has already made four commitments to funds in Asia, according to a well-placed *AVCJ* source.

By asset class, two of the investments were in funds focusing on venture capital, one was in buyout, and the remaining commitment went to a fund concentrated on growth stage deals. The funds are all in North Asia, specifically China, Korea, and Japan.

The fund of funds has recently set up shop in Hong Kong and also has a Beijing representative office and a small office in San Francisco.

Anchor investors in Asia Alternatives are Oak Hill Investment Management, Hellman & Friedman (Ma's former firm), and Silicon Valley's iconic Arthur Rock.   *- RAF*

296

Reflections on A Changed Life

ROSLYN BRAEMAN PAYNE (MBA 1970), PRESIDENT, JACKSON STREET PARTNERS, SAN FRANCISCO, CALIFORNIA

In February 1986, I was selected to be the first CEO of the Federal Asset Disposition Association, a government-sponsored entity tasked with managing

assets from failed savings and loans. I was chosen because I had the required skill set: management experience, real-estate knowledge, and a background in both asset management and property development. However, what I lacked was experience in navigating through the political environment of Washington, DC.

Although I created a professional team and approached the task with discipline and a determination to save the taxpayer's pocketbook, I failed. I was unable to stop the powerful financial interests that wanted to buy assets at ten cents on the dollar—and knew how to accomplish their goals. As a result, there was, in my estimation, an unnecessary $100 billion loss to the American taxpayer. I had learned by experience the power of vested interests in Washington, and resigned after two years.

Yet despite my failure, I had acquired a deep understanding of capital markets and poor federal policies and decided to focus my business efforts on investing in the arena of residential real estate. (It was clear to me that there would be capital shortages, but I believed in the continuing presence of a strong demand for housing.) I exited this investment plan in 2005 when it became apparent that the markets were overextended, but my earlier failure had laid the groundwork for a very successful next chapter of my career.

———

CATHERINE BOUVIER D'YVOIRE (MBA 1982), FINANCIAL ADVISOR TO GOVERNMENTS, PARIS, FRANCE

After years of working "happily" in the same company, I failed at transitioning from one boss to the next. My new boss did not acknowledge my work. The value I created was not "visible": The goodwill I had been creating with my clients through hard work was not valued nor attributed to me.

I learned from the experience that you should not let anyone take credit for your work; by the same token that you take responsibility for your mistakes, take ownership of your contribution. Be visible. Make sure your seniors know what you do, especially if some of your work is intangible. Managing your boss and seniors is as important as managing your team and peers. In a changing environment, identify the game's new rules and players and switch gears ASAP.

———

BENNIE WILEY (MBA 1972), PRINCIPAL, WILEY GROUP, BROOKLINE, MASSACHUSETTS

One of my favorite ventures was a toy store I created on Martha's Vineyard. I loved everything about the store: the quality of the products we sold, the children and families we served, and the pleasure and developmental benefit we brought to our customers. My original plan was to gain expertise and brand with the Martha's Vineyard store, then expand to sites in the Boston area and at other resort communities. Unfortunately, this never happened—partly because the economy took a downturn, but also because I did not yet have the knowledge and resources I later developed. The toy business, like every industry, has its unique features, and as I had never before worked in it, I had not yet formed connections with people who could have helped me better navi-

LAURE WANG (MBA 1997), COFOUNDER AND MANAGING DIRECTOR, ASIA ALTERNATIVES, ATHERTON, CALIFORNIA

Earlier in my life, I chose not to apply to Harvard for my undergraduate education because I thought I wasn't good enough to get accepted. I subsequently was accepted at Yale, MIT, and Stanford, where I enrolled and had a great education. But the experience taught me to persevere and not give up without trying hard. I used this experience when starting Asia Alternatives (even though I was afraid to launch a start-up) and now, with my stroke, I am trying to defy all odds and get better.

(Editor's note: Wang suffered a stem cell stroke in 2010 and is a quadriplegic mute with "locked-in syndrome." She uses eye-tracking technology to communicate by computer and to operate a motorized wheelchair. Wang remains active with investments and deal sourcing at her firm and in raising her two young sons with her husband, Kabir Misra.)

Forum review

PE Leaders' Summit
22nd Annual AVCJ Private Equity & Venture Forum

11 November 2009

Global perspective, local opportunities

Four Seasons Hotel, Hong Kong

Sponsors

ALLEN & OVERY

ALTER DOMUS

Mourant

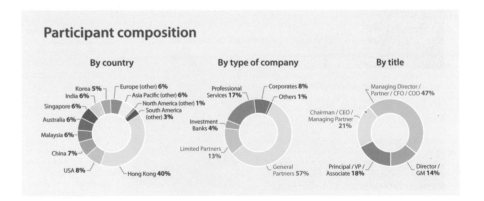

Participant composition

By country

Korea **5%**
India **6%**
Singapore **6%**
Australia **6%**
Malaysia **6%**
China **7%**
USA **8%**
Europe (other) **6%**
Asia Pacific (other) **6%**
North America (other) **1%**
South America (other) **3%**
Hong Kong **40%**

By type of company

Professional Services **17%**
Corporates **8%**
Others **1%**
Investment Banks **4%**
Limited Partners **13%**
General Partners **57%**

By title

Managing Director / Partner / CFO / COO **47%**
Chairman / CEO / Managing Partner **21%**
Principal / VP / Associate **18%**
Director / GM **14%**

PE Leaders' Summit 2009

November 11th 2009 | Four Seasons Hotel, Hong Kong

AVCJ's PE Leaders' Summit is a focused one-day forum especially tailored to address the day-to-day business and operational issues facing the managers of private equity funds across Asia.

150 participants from more than **90** companies and **17** countries

Well attended with a **good mix of industry professionals.**

DAVID EDWARDS
LaSalle Investment Management

Speakers

James Ahn, *Partner & Head of McKinsey's Asia-Pacific Mergers & Acquisitions Practice,* **MCKINSEY & COMPANY**
Fredrik Åtting , *Sr. Partner,* **EQT PARTNERS ASIA LTD**
Vinit Bhatia, *Partner, Co-Head of Private Equity Group for Greater China,* **BAIN & COMPANY**
Brian Bunker, *Managing Director, Asia,* **RIVERSIDE ASIA PARTNERS**
Carlo Caiani, *Executive Director,* **CAIANI & COMPANY PTY LTD**
Doug Coulter, *Head of Private Equity, Asia Pacific,* **LGT CAPITAL PARTNERS**
Shiv Dalvie, *Managing Director,* **AEA INVESTORS LLC**
Ray Haarstick, *CEO & Founder,* **RELEVANT EQUITY SYSTEMS**
Chris Hasson, *CEO,* **JOHNSON ELECTRIC CAPITAL**
Dominic Jones, *Managing Director,* **ALTER DOMUS**
Jae-Woo Lee, *Founding Partner,* **VOGO FUND**
Tim Mann, *Head of Asia Fund Administration,* **MOURANT**
Will McAuliffe, *Partner,* **ALLEN & OVERY**
Brian M. McDaniel, *Partner,* **GOODWIN PROCTER LLP**
Liang Meng, *CEO, Greater China Private Equity,* **D.E. SHAW**
Rodney Muse, *Co-Founder & Managing Partner,* **NAVIS CAPITAL PARTNERS**
Harish Parameswar, *Managing Director, Asia,* **LAZARD ASIA LIMITED**
Mark Qiu, *CEO & Managing Director,* **CHINA RENAISSANCE CAPITAL INVESTMENT INC**
Brett Rochkind, *Principal,* **GENERAL ATLANTIC**
Johannes Schoeter, *Founding Partner,* **CHINA NEW ENTERPRISE INVESTMENT**
David Shen, *Managing Director,* **OLYMPUS CAPITAL HOLDINGS ASIA**
Jagannadham Thunuguntla, *Equity Head,* **SMC CAPITALS LIMITED**
Sebastiaan van den Berg, *Principal,* **HARBOURVEST PARTNERS (ASIA) LIMITED**
Kanad S. Virk, *COO,* **STANDARD CHARTERED IL&FS ASIA INFRASTRUCTURE GROWTH FUND**
Laure Wang, *Co-Founder & Managing Director,* **ASIA ALTERNATIVES**

Over the last 20 years I have had 5 momentous occasions:

First was my marriage to Kabir Misra in Kauai. He is my best friend and biggest supporter. Kabir went to Harvard undergraduate and the GSB for his MBA. We just celebrated our 8th anniversary.

Second, having Marat (nicknamed Ton-Ton), is 6 going on 60. He is super smart and loves reading Harry Potter. He started at Bing and is now attending First Grade at Sacred Heart. Sacred Heart goes until the 12th Grade, so no more interviews!

Third, having Madyn (nicknamed Caillou), he is two and a free spirit. He goes to Bing and loves Stanford. He is always smiling and dancing. I am happy to see both of my children grow.

Fourth, in 2006, I founded Asia Alternatives with my partners Melissa and Rebecca who I knew from Goldman Sachs and HBS, respectively. Asia Alternatives was one of the earliest dedicated Asia private equity fund of funds. Today, we manage almost $4 billion, making Asia Alternatives the largest player in this space. I am proud to continue to help lead the Firm as a Co Founder and Senior Advisor.

Fifth, was having a brain stem stroke. It affects my verbal communication, but not my mind. I am still the same but I have Locked-In Syndrome. Don't treat me with pity because I am grateful to be alive. My stroke has taught me patience and faith. In college, my nickname was "Spaz". How ironic that I now have uncontrolled muscles spasms after the stroke. They remind me that I am blessed.

I have a great husband, two beautiful kids, a thriving business which are all testaments to my luck. I am happy to participate in this reunion and I hope that I will see you at reunions to come.

Laure Wang

ASIA ALTERNATIVES

EMBARGOED UNTIL 6 PM EST ON 4/14/15 / 6 AM CHINA TIME ON 4/15/15 / 7 AM JAPAN TIME ON 4/15/15

Asia Alternatives Announces Fund Closings of over US$1.8 billion

Hong Kong, Beijing, Shanghai and San Francisco—April 14/15, 2015—Asia Alternatives, one of the largest independent Asian private equity fund-of-funds, today announced the final close of over US$1.8 billion in new commitments across Asia Alternatives Capital Partners IV, LP ("AACP IV") and its related fund vehicles ("Fund IV").

"We are extremely grateful that a significant number of our original limited partners continue to support us and we are pleased to have added a number of highly respected and well-recognized new investors in Fund IV," said Melissa Ma, Co-Founder and Managing Director of Asia Alternatives.

The largest of the Funds is Asia Alternatives Capital Partners IV, LP which, along with its sleeve fund focused on investments outside Japan, AACP IV Ex-Japan Investors, LP, closed on US$1 billion of committed capital, above their combined target of US$750 million. AACP IV is the successor fund to Asia Alternatives Capital Partners III, LP ("AACP III"), which closed in July 2012. Earlier funds include Asia Alternatives Capital Partners II, LP ("AACP II"), which closed in September 2008, and Asia Alternatives Capital Partners, LP ("AACP I"), which closed in May 2007.

The Fund IV closings totaling over US$1.8 billion represent an approximate 20% increase over the last announced fund closings in August 2012 of over US$1.5 billion across AACP III and its related fund vehicles.

"In the 10th year since our founding, Asia Alternatives is proud of the strong partnerships we have formed with both our investors across the world and with our fund managers across China, India, Japan, Korea, South East Asia and Australia. The Asia private equity ecosystem has developed well over the last decade and we look to further growth for years to come," Ma continued.

The Funds are focused on building a diversified portfolio with an emphasis on top-performing local Asian fund managers. Asia Alternatives invests in Greater China, Japan, Korea, South East Asia, India and Australia and across buyout, growth, venture capital and special situations funds. The firm has invested in over 40 managers in Asia since inception.

ASIA ALTERNATIVES

"Portfolio construction is a critical focus at Asia Alternatives, as we seek risk diversification across geographies, strategies and managers that we actively monitor. The opportunity set for Asia private equity is continuously evolving and we intend to capitalize on those investments that provide the best risk-adjusted returns," Ma concluded.

Approximately 80% of investors in AACP IV were from pre-existing relationships in AACP III, AACP II and AACP I. Investors in the Funds represent a global pool of private capital sources, such as state and corporate pension funds, foundations, university endowments, insurance companies and family offices in the United States, Canada, Europe and Asia. Institutional investors across all Fund IV vehicles include Cathay Life Insurance Co., Comprehensive Financial Management, Florida State Board of Administration, Jasper Ridge Partners, Massachusetts Mutual Life Insurance Company, New York State Common Retirement Fund, San Francisco City and County Employees' Retirement System, Teachers' Retirement System of the State of Illinois, University of Missouri, University of Vermont and Virginia Retirement System.

Asia Alternatives is one of the first independently formed Asian private equity fund-of-funds. The firm also received the first Limited Partner QFLP (Qualified Foreign Limited Partner) license in China, which allowed Asia Alternatives to invest in selected, qualified RMB-denominated private equity investments.

Eaton Partners, LLC acted as exclusive placement agent for Asia Alternatives and Pillsbury Winthrop Shaw Pittman LLP served as legal counsel.

About Asia Alternatives Management LLC
Asia Alternatives is a solution platform dedicated to helping institutional investors make investments in private equity across Asia. The firm was founded in 2005 by Melissa Ma, Laure Wang and Rebecca Xu. Asia Alternatives is currently managing Asia Alternatives Capital Partners, LP ($515 million), Asia Alternatives Capital Partners II, LP ($950 million), Asia Alternatives Capital Partners III, LP ($908 million) and Asia Alternatives Capital Partners IV, LP and AACP IV Ex-Japan Investors, LP (collectively $1 billion) and other funds, all of which are Asia-focused private equity funds-of-funds. The firm has over $6.5 billion in assets under management.

Asia Alternatives invests with top performing private equity fund managers across Asia primarily in Greater China (Mainland China, Taiwan, and Hong Kong), Japan, Korea, South East Asia, India and Australia and that are diversified across buyout, growth and expansion, venture capital and special situations funds. The firm

currently has over 35 professionals across offices in Hong Kong, Beijing, Shanghai and San Francisco. For more information, please visit www.asiaalternatives.com.

This press release does not constitute the offer of advisory services or offer of a security or the solicitation of an investment.

###

For More Information:

Investor Contact:
Melissa J. Ma – Co-Founder & Managing Director
Asia Alternatives Management LLC
Tel: (415) 723-8101
mma@asiaalt.com

Media Contact:
Steve Bruce/Taylor Ingraham/John Stavinga
ASC Advisors LLC
Tel: (203) 992-1230
sbruce@ascadvisors.com; tingraham@ascadvisors.com; jstavinga@ascadvisors.com

Media Contact for Asia Ex-Japan:
Richard Barton/Grace Zhang
Newgate Communications
Tel: (852)3758 2606 / (852)3758 2687
richard.barton@newgate.asia; grace.zhang@newgate.asia

Media Contact for Japan:
Deborah Hayden/Ginger Lin
Edelman
Tel: (813)4360 9000
Deborah.hayden@edelman.com; ginger.lin@edelman.com

Acknowledgements

I want to thank Hildy Augustin for helping me reach conclusions for each chapter and for helping me to change from depression to joy. I also want to thank Brian Madigan for giving me the idea of a preface. I am grateful to my caregivers who suffered through the frustrations of the dynavox while I wrote this book. Thank you to Vanessa Rocha, Natasha Papa, Nayell Torres, and Yolanda Mancias for helping me execute edits. I am indebted to Patty Tung Gaw for her smart editing. I also want to thank Erin Ganju, Amy Su, and Francis Tapon for helping me find a publisher in the United States. Thanks to Berta Garcia and Claudia Wagner for scanning pictures and articles. I want to thank Kyung Kim for putting on her paralegal hat and Denise Garcia for relaying those edits. I am grateful for Fabiola Salvador for her quarterbacking United States efforts, and Ellen Tsai for all her time and effort during the whole process. Lastly, I want to say thank you to my father, Paul Wang, for my tenth year anniversary gift of compiling, printing, and publishing this book in Taiwan.

Laure L. Wang

Reflections on A Changed Life

Laure L. Wang 王樂怡

Publisher: Pacific Venture Partners 怡和創業投資集團
Address: 8F-2, 351, Yang Guang Street, Taipei, Taiwan
TEL: 8862-2797-9877
FAX: 8862-2797-0377
Art Editor: United Daily News Pre-press/Production Dep.
Printing: United Daily News Production Dep.
        3F, No.369, Sec.1, Datong Rd., Xizhi Dist., New
        Taipei City 22161, Taiwan（R.O.C.）
TEL: 8862-8692-5588

First Edition: September, 2015
ISBN: 978-986-87771-2-5（平裝）

Reflections on A Changed Life